A Knock at the Door

Forty Miscellaneous Meditations

Colin Evans

ISBN 0 85346 239 9

© Colin Evans, 2005

Published by
Granary Press
the imprint of the United Reformed Church
86 Tavistock Place, London WC1H 9RT

Produced by Communications and Editorial, Graphics Office

Printed by Healeys Printers, Unit 10, The Sterling Complex,
Farthing Road, Ipswich, Suffolk IP1 5AP

By the same author:

A MONTH OF SUNDAYS

A HANDFUL OF MINUTES

COMMUNICATE OR DIE
The United Reformed Church Book, 1985

THE MIRROR AND THE SKYLIGHT
The Reflections of a Stage-Struck Vicar

For Margaret

My dear wife and 'carer'

CONTENTS

Continued overleaf ...

Words of explanation

For well over forty years in a varied ministry of the Word, in pulpits, before TV cameras, at studio microphones and through many a printed sheet, I have poured out millions of words. I know something of what T S Eliot meant when in *East Coker* he wrote of 'the intolerable wrestle with words and meanings'.

Of what use mine have been, I cannot tell. Can any of them, I dare to speculate, be of any further use if selected, rearranged and served up in some other slightly more permanent form? I entertain no such grandiose ambitions as the afflicted Job had when he cried: 'How I wish that someone would remember my words and record them in a book! Or with a chisel carve my words in stone and write them so that they would last for ever.' (Job 19: 23-4 GNB) I simply wish to share with a wider audience thoughts and insights which have come my way over these years, and have been imparted like puffs of instantly dissolving smoke in sermons, through broadcasts, in quickly forgotten journals and, not least, in four books thus far. I am immensely grateful to Carol Rogers, Secretary for Communications, who has encouraged me to set down the forty miscellaneous meditations in this fifth book. Also, to our graphic designer Sara Foyle, my gratitude for her imaginative design of a door to fit the overall title of the book, and to convey the atmosphere of Holman Hunt's famous painting in the essay carrying the same title on pages 73-76.

I make no heady claim to be an originator, only a mediator. My debt to so many others for the enlightenment they have brought me is enormous. The desire to write is a kind of painful obsession. I empathise with Carla Carlisle, an American over here who farms in Suffolk and has written regularly for *Country Life*. 'When one kind reader,' she said, 'wrote that my column reads "like you love writing", I could only reply guiltily, "Nope, what I love is *having written*." '

The pieces in this coffee table or bedside collection are intended for easy reading. Their format is the devotional essay, their objective the communication of the

Christian faith. They may even provide ideas and illustrations for preachers, teachers, and public speakers. Feel free, if you are such, to take what you want and leave what you don't.

Since 1996 I have been a regular columnist for *REFORM*, and I owe many thanks to its editor David Lawrence for so freely entrusting me with a monthly page (except in September, when the edition is entirely taken up by comprehensive reportage of the United Reformed Church General Assembly). I stress that none of the pieces in this collection are repeats of any I have contributed to *REFORM*. They are all freshly minted, and are a bit longer.

Alpheton, Suffolk
March 2005
CGE

1

Does it really matter?

I can hear the laughter echoing around those Galilean hills. His contemporaries must often have laughed at the verbal pictures Jesus drew in his teaching. Matthew 23 contains his criticism of the law-makers of Jerusalem who had fanatically reduced general regulations into precise rules of the most detailed and trivial kind.

Take the law about tithing. It stated that ten per cent of the produce of a man's land must be offered to God. But Jesus fiercely ridicules their demand that the smallest items from one's back garden like mint, for example, are subject to this law as well as the main crops from the fields. 'Alas for you, scribes and Pharisees, hypocrites!' he says to them. 'You pay tithes of mint and dill and cumin; but you have overlooked the weightier demands of the law – justice, mercy, and good faith.' Then he goes on to call them blind guides. 'You strain off a midge, yet gulp down a camel!' he concludes; and what a picture that is! I daresay he made gestures to add to the fun. What a task it must have been to slice up the exact amount of mint to offer to the priests at the temple.

The Pharisees were also scrupulous in the extreme about cleanliness, both general and ritual. They habitually strained their wine through a sieve. The picture is of a man sitting down to his meal and meticulously straining out a tiny insect from his glass of wine but cheerfully eating a filthy great animal for lunch. It is a grossly exaggerated picture, of course. A cartoon, in fact.

It is a classical joke which has often been repeated by the world's funny men. Chaplin did it in *The Gold Rush* when he made elaborate preparations at the meal table, put on a bib and proceeded to eat a dirty old boot as though sitting in the Dorchester or the Waldorf.

Jesus pleads for a sense of proportion. Does it really matter? How many of us, I wonder, are daily faced with much that doesn't. The bishop came to breakfast one morning when Hugh Montefiore, later to be episcopally distinguished himself, was there as a youthful curate. Being young and rather nervous in the august presence of a bishop, he upset the teapot over the table. It happened in a flash. What a calamity in such company! And afterwards, an enraged wife to settle with too, no doubt. But the bishop saved the day with a wise and comforting remark. As the tablecloth rapidly changed colour, like litmus paper in the chemistry lab, his lordship said quietly, 'Now is the time of think of eternity!' In other words, let's get this mishap in proportion. It's made a bit of a mess and perhaps spoiled a nice tablecloth, but *does it really matter?*

We can ask that question *at home.*

I have occasionally visited homes where I have felt I oughtn't to be there. I might muddy the carpets, or pollute the settee with hairs from my dog, or stain a tabletop with a spot from my coffee cup. I have know housewives who expect visitors to remove their footwear before entering. Like Moses at the burning bush, they stand there as if on holy ground. So, a house ceases to be a home and becomes an end in itself. We are reminded of Hyacinth Bucket, Roy Clarke's astonishing character who lives by a totally false sense of values in the ever repeatable TV sitcom *Keeping Up Appearances.* She drives her nervous next-door neighbour to spill the cup of coffee every time simply because the poor woman is frightened of doing just that in the presence of a pathologically houseproud monster.

Burt Bacharach wrote a soulful tune to Hal David's sad lyric in which a man's wife has left him. The gist of it is that a chair is not a chair when there's no one sitting there. And a chair is not a house, and a house is not a home, when there's no one there. A home is people not things. When a fire breaks out, the rescue of persons is what matters.'

A great Methodist leader and preacher of our own time, Dr Will Sangster, once wrote: 'Material things … are all in their minor place with the saint and no more important than the furnishings of an inn. Who cares much whether it is pseudo-Chippendale or Sheraton? We are only staying for the night.'

Does it really matter? We can ask that question of *society at large*.

What folly rules the world of humankind! I mean, in regard to such paltry matters as status, money, possessions, class. Utter nonsense is talked about status symbols like houses in superior neighbourhoods, and the ownership of a particular type of car. The Ford Motor Company some years ago marketed an imitation 'posh' car known as the Capri so that we can all join the 'set' and become among 'the people who count'.

I read recently about Grace Kelly's father. He and his family were dragged into the news when his film-star daughter became engaged to Prince Rainier. John B Kelly owned the largest building construction firm in the USA. One press article told us that Mr Kelly was especially thrilled because he had started out in life in a small way as a bricklayer. It so happened that he was also an excellent oarsman. Nevertheless, because he was at the time a manual worker he was disqualified from rowing at the Henley Regatta. When you consider the tawdry philosophy lying behind his disqualification, how despicable it looks. And what does it really matter even if the Kelly family did marry into royalty? What counts is not that Grace became a princess but that she loved her husband and had that love returned. What kind of ethic is it that downgrades a man whose skill lies in his hands and whose livelihood is obtained from them?

Presumably they wouldn't have allowed Jesus to row at Henley because he was a carpenter. Nor Paul, who also had a trade on the side as a tent-maker, although perhaps his intellectual prowess might have got him in. Peter, Andrew, James and John wouldn't have stood much chance, their brawny hands smelling of fish. Matthew, however, whose hands were once dirty with corrupt tax-collecting for the enemy, would have been acceptable, we suppose. He was a white-collared worker, a civil servant. What folly rules the world of humankind! Class, status, possessions – does it really matter?

We can ask that question *in the Church*.

We church folk seem to be experts in midge-straining and camel-swallowing. We make overmuch of matters which have nothing whatever to do with the life of the ordinary man in the street waiting to board the Clapham omnibus. Lord

Soper of blessed memory criticised the Methodist Conference, trying to imagine what a casual observer sitting in the gallery would make of it all. 'I am bound to say,' he stated, 'that unless the casual observer was a devoted Christian he would feel that we were making pious noises in peculiar places while the world rolled by.'

How much of what we do in our assemblies and meetings and conferences really matters? Who among our ministers has no tale to tell about church meetings where forty precious minutes are taken up with an argument about where to store a dozen chairs, or what colour to paint the church kitchen, or why we should change the time of the morning service.

When Kenneth Slack ministered at the City Temple, he urged his people to maintain a right perspective on the affairs of the church's day-to-day life. He said some sharp words. 'Miss Jones has stopped coming to church because she doesn't like the size of the cross in the apse. Mr Smith is not coming any more because he was not re-elected on to that committee. Mr Ponsonby says he "doesn't believe in Foreign Missions", and he won't come any more because a recent sermon on India made him uncomfortable and he called it "disgusting". Mrs Thompson, her husband tells me, sobbed herself to sleep because she was not asked to pour out the tea …' Bold Kenneth!

What, then, does really matter? The simple answer is harmony, a relationship of responsive goodwill towards our fellows and with our God. I'd better stop there, before I become an unstoppable, running tap of pious clichés.

2

The grasshopper complex

In childhood I was always fascinated by tales about giants. And this especially when Rupert Bear trespassed on to a giant's estate and almost fell into his huge hands. At Christmas, of course, there was from year to year the pantomime about Jack's Beanstalk with a giant at the top of it. I was awed by Bunyan's Giant Despair. In these latter years, studying the myths of folklore, I have been surprised at the number of legendary giants there have been in our islands.

The giant who threatened Hampshire was disposed of by Sir Bevis. In Leicestershire the giant Bel died in a riding accident. Bolster was one of the Cornish giants, tricked to his death. There was even a husband-and-wife team of outsize beings who were supposed to have built St Michael's Mount. The fierce Red Etin in Scottish border country had all three of his heads chopped off, and Jack the Giant Killer was invited to a seat at King Arthur's Round Table. I am particularly partial to the Wrekin Giant who wanted to flood the town of Shrewsbury by damming the Severn. He was dissuaded from doing so, but the giant spadeful of earth he had intended to use was left to become that so-called craggy hill known as the Wrekin near Oswestry.

Now, open your Bible, and you'll find giants haunting its earlier pages. In Genesis chapter six, we read that 'there were giants in the earth in those days'. They were the Nephilim who must have been unusually tall and rugged men, and the Anakim who were believed to have been the offspring from a union of the 'sons of God with the daughters of men'.

Long before we get to Goliath, young David's Philistine opponent (for whom I have some sympathy!), there are the giants of Canaan. In Numbers 13 and 14, we read of the reconnaissance party appointed by Moses in infiltrate the Canaanite country, their Promised Land, before he and his nomadic escapees from Egypt launched the invasion. The party consisted of 12 members, one from each tribe. They are all named, as if to authenticate the claim that it really happened.

Moses gave them a detailed briefing. Let them check the nature of the territory, observe the strengths and weaknesses of the inhabitants, gather population statistics and find out whether the towns were open or fortified. Was the land fertile or barren or wooded? They were to bring back some sample fruit. As it was the season of ripe grapes, it must have been the end of July. The spies carried on a pole a large bunch of grapes to take back, with pomegranate and figs.

After forty days, the 'recce' was completed. They must have journeyed as much as sixty miles from the encampment. Now, however, their report was at hand. It was discouraging.

Yes, it was a fruitful, fertile land certainly; but its inhabitants looked formidable. Their towns and villages were very large and fortified, with walls 12 to 15 feet thick and 30 to 50 feet high. *And there were giants there.*

Caleb, son of Jephunneh, from the tribe of Judah, was the odd man out among the spies. 'Let us go up at once and occupy the country,' he said, 'we are well able to conquer it.' He would have met with the approval of Mirabeau, the eighteenth century French revolutionary politician. 'Impossible?' he said when someone used the word concerning one of his projects. 'Never mention to me again that blockhead of a word.' Unhappily, the lone Caleb was shouted down. 'The country we explored,' they said, 'will swallow up any who go to live in it. All the people we saw there are men of gigantic stature: *we felt no bigger than grasshoppers.*'

Giants and grasshoppers! The big and the tiny! The strong and the weak!

My researches inform me that no archaeological evidence for people of abnormal stature has ever been found in the Near East. All the talk about giants was probably based on the assumption that only giants could have built the walls of the ancient cities, in Greece as well as in Canaan. The archaeologists of old made the mistake of thinking that the remains they dug up of fantastically tall beings must have been human, and that the height of humankind was patently decreasing. In truth, the opposite is the case. In our village hall at social functions, we can hardly help but observe that there men and women who tower over us in their exceptional height. At Lucerne in 1577, a 19ft skeleton was discovered and assumed at the time to be human. Other such finds over the centuries have exposed measurements ranging from 30ft to 90ft, and in the fourteenth century the remains of a monster measuring 300ft found in Sicily could hardly have been those of a man.

The exciting story of the Canaan reconnaissance points us to *the problem of exaggeration*. The children of Israel, free from confinement in Egypt but wandering and as yet of no fixed abode, exaggerated both ways. *They magnified their difficulties and minimized their powers.*

This is the essence of what we may term the Grasshopper Complex.

Suppose, however, we reverse the process and say, 'They minimized their difficulties and magnified their powers'.

There are two kinds of people: those who underestimate their ability to cope with jobs whose difficulties they exaggerate; and those who are resolutely confident that they can surmount a challenge which they refuse to allow to get them down. The two types are well-illustrated in a conversation that Beverley Nichols once had with Winston Churchill.

The author had just had his first real success with a novel entitled *Prelude*. Churchill asked him how long it had taken him to write it. Nichols explained that he'd done it in fitful spasms over about five months. But didn't he go to his desk every morning and write? demanded Winston. Well, no. He had to wait for the right mood and inspiration. 'Nonsense!' growled the old bulldog. 'You should go to your room every morning at nine o'clock and say, "I'm going to write for four hours".' Beverley Nichols asked about such interferences as toothache, indigestion and sheer lethargy. 'You've got to get over that.' replied Churchill unsympathetically. If you sit waiting for inspiration, you will sit waiting until you are an old man. Writing is like any job – like marching an army, for instance. If you sit down and wait until the weather is fine, you won't get far with your troops. Kick yourself, irritate yourself, but <u>write</u>; it's the only way.'

It is fatally easy to slump under the Grasshopper Complex, to moan that the job, whatever it is, is impossible, and one just hasn't the ability to cope.

'Your faith is too small,' said Jesus to his men. Then he went on to talk about moving mountains. He was here employing a familiar metaphor often used by the teacher who could solve testing problems and resolve troublesome difficulties. Such was known as a pulveriser or uprooter of mountains. Power, sheer power! 'The kingdom of God is not a matter of talk but of power,' wrote Paul to Corinth (1 Corinthians 4: 20). To his Philippian friends he testified to the flow of that power in his own life. 'I have strength for anything,' he wrote, 'though him who gives me power' (4: 13). See what he, a diminutive man nearer to a grasshopper than to a giant, who shook and trembled with nerves whenever he had to speak in public, was enabled to achieve across a stormy Mediterranean world.

I like that card seen in an Eastbourne jeweller's shop: 'There is nothing we may not hope to repair.' It's the Caleb spirit.

3

The scandal of the specific

The Bible doesn't whitewash its heroes. Or should I say, its anti-heroes? They are clay-footed, terribly human. Angels perhaps, but often angels with dirty faces. Take King David, for example. To steal Bathsheba, the wife of Uriah the Hittite, an officer in David's army, he arranged for the man to be exposed to certain death on the battlefield. The deadly ploy worked, Uriah was killed, and his wife became the King's.

Along comes Nathan the prophet who tells David a story about a rich man with large flocks who steals a poor man's only sheep, which ends up on the rich man's dinner table. The story angers David who says, 'The man who did this deserves to die!' Nathan said to David, 'You are the man!' The case is fully presented, like a report in a Sunday tabloid, in 2 Samuel chapters 11 and 12. The account could be described as an example of 'the scandal of the specific'.

With such a phrase, we hit upon a major problem for preachers.

How direct and honest to God can we be? The worldly-wise advise us to be tactful, discreet and diplomatic. These a minister must be, if he is to retain his congregation. Let him not speak too directly, too honestly, too personally. Yet the biblical prophets did. Take the scathing denunciations of Amos, who thundered against the sins of Israel at a time of much prosperity and plentiful piety. But such fierce and frank speaking often led to suffering and death. The consequence of John the Baptist's blunt condemnation of Herod to his face led to John's beheading; and Stephen's long speech to the Council in Jerusalem decided his fate by judicial stoning.

the man.' The photos God takes are not only of wide sweeps of scenery and of milling crowds of nameless individuals. They are portraits of people one by one in close-up.

I learn that my own concern for others should follow the same principle. William Blake summed it up for us in two lines.

> *He who would do good to another must do it in Minute Particulars:*
> *General good is the plea of the Scoundrel, hypocrite and flatterer.*

God doesn't say: 'Do good', he says, 'Give a cup of cold water to that man who is desperately thirsty, that man over there in the grey coat and large brown hat.'

4

The words of advent

The press release informed us that the Bishop was planning to lead a Quiet Day during the first week in Advent. It would start with coffee at ten (always welcome), and the day would be divided into four sessions. Under the title 'Putting Last Things First', the Bishop promised to take a new look at four Advent themes: Death, Judgement, Hell and Heaven.

Is Advent the right time to ponder such sombre subjects? Most of the season's words are words of joyful welcome. Hark, the glad sound! The Saviour comes … Joy to the world … joy of every longing heart … Wake, O wake! with tidings thrilling … Rejoice! Rejoice! These are the dominant words of Advent.

Advent is a time to dwell on LIFE

Childbirth is an uneasy mixture of eager expectation and panicky anxiety. Bethlehem echoes with rejoicing at the birth in the stable, but it also re-echoes with the sound of 'sobbing in bitter grief' after Herod's demand for a massacre of infants has been done. Evil stalked abroad then and still does today; and children, tiny children, go on being abused, maimed and murdered.

Soon after Advent we celebrate the Christmas birth and exult in the gift of life, new life, life renewed, lives redeemed. But people die, and newly born babies lose life, even on Christmas Day itself.

An Anglican clergyman came into the BBC studios in Gloucester to record four short stories he had written in a book recalling his life as a vicar in East Anglia. I planned to transmit them on the four Sundays of Advent in 1993. He and his wife had three children. They were getting on well, aged 22, 19 and 8. There had been a fourth, born grievously defective in 1977. The little mite, baptised by his father just before he died, lived only five hours.

John, the father, warned me that towards the end of recording the last of his stories, he might break down. He did, sobbing heavily. It was the poem, really a prayer his wife had written at the time of their loss, that did it for John. We waited for him to recover, and bravely and unwaveringly he read the prayer. It was a confirmation that the trite saying that 'time will heal' isn't true. We recall Edna St Vincent Millay's agonised cry

> Time does not bring relief, you all have lied
> Who told me time would ease me of my pain!

John and his wife Diana still felt the intense pain of their loss even 16 years on.

We tread softly, then. There are hurt people all around us. Still, the invocation is for the Lord of the dawning Dayspring to 'come and cheer our spirits, disperse the gloomy clouds of night, and death's dark shadows put to flight'. Bernard Shaw said: 'Life is a flame that is always burning itself out, but it catches fire again every time a child is born.'

Advent is a time to emphasise COMPASSION

The historian Noel Annan, born in 1916 and writing of his own generation in 1990, declared that the cardinal virtue was no longer to love one's country. It was 'to feel compassion for one's fellow men and women'. The word means *practical* pity, the kind which is not merely a matter of words but, my dictionary informs me, is 'an inclination to help or be merciful'.

The Gospels tell us that Jesus was 'moved with compassion'. He felt for the worried and helpless, living as they were, under foreign occupation; and he showed compassion for a leper, an untouchable, by deliberately touching him. The Samaritan hero in his most popular parable had compassion of the most practical kind for the Jew mugged and left to die beside the Jericho road. He acted like a paramedic, dressing the poor man's wounds; and then, putting him on his donkey, he took him as if by ambulance to a wayside inn where, like a BUPA client, he personally paid for the man's nursing back to health.

I had a senior colleague in the ministry in my own early days who, in preparing to celebrate Christmas each year, made a point of re-reading *A Christmas Carol*. Once Advent had begun, he would seek out his well-worn copy and read that golden tale in which Dickens perfectly reflected the teaching of Jesus. Scrooge 'saw the light', stopped shouting Bah! Humbug! And expressed his new understanding of Christmas by his compassion toward the poor Cratchits, calling on them with generous favours, such as the biggest turkey in town.

Advent is a time to acknowledge PLEASURE

The Welsh poet, R S Thomas, wrote of Protestantism as 'the adroit castrator of art; the bitter negation of song and dance and the heart's innocent joy'. He accused the uptight Calvinists of having 'botched our flesh and left us only the soul's terrible impotence in a warm world'.

The very word 'pleasure', particularly when related to sex and our sexuality, has for long enough been a problem in the Christian tradition. The Old Testament book Song of Songs is a lyrical poem about carnal love, a frank exposition of lovemaking, the Lord's own sex manual. It was noticeably left out of the old lectionaries. Biblical scholars of the past insisted on treating it as an allegory pointing to God's dealings with his beloved Israel, all on a high spiritual plane.

John Fowles, in his novel *The French Lieutenant's Woman*, created Mrs Poulteney, the plump Victorian vulture of Lyme Regis. She had a large family Bible on her lectern in the corner of her drawing room, 'from which certain inexplicable errors of taste in the Holy Writ (such as the Song of Songs) had been piously excised'.

Fortunately we are growing out of such unhealthy prudery, which has no place in the Judaeo-Christian community.

With the birth of the Bethlehem Babe, may we not celebrate in pleasurable ways? 'Your presence fills me with joy,' said the Psalmist, 'and brings me pleasure for ever.'

Advent is a time to be thankful for EARTH

There are those who think that Christianity has all to do with heaven, and nothing to do with earth, the earthly or even the earthy. God is restricted to heaven, and the purpose of life is to get to God in heaven which is all good, and to reject earth which is all bad. We are all affected, it is claimed, by the conflict between our spiritual nature and our so-called 'lower nature'.

When in October 1954 I was inducted to the pastorate at Ilkley in Yorkshire, a large burly man, a fellow Welshman as it happened, stood up to speak. He looked as if he had played a lot of rugby. He was an MP, if my memory is still functioning. He made it clear that I must not preach politics; and he reminded me that my job had to do with heaven, and that all earthly matters should be left to him and his colleagues at Westminster. Heaven help us, I thought!

The creed which claims that God's realm is entirely celestial isn't Christianity. It is a third-century heresy known as Manichaeism named after its founder Mani, or Manichaeus, who first preached it on 20 March in AD 242. It was influential for a thousand years, spreading east and west, and there are still traces of it in many places.

Intermingled with this heresy is the popular, half-joking view that life in heaven must be monotonous and boring. It's time for a laugh.

The Yorkshireman arrived at the Pearly Gates. Out came the Recording Angel who, wearily unlocking them, says: 'From Yorkshire, eh? Well, yer can come in, but yer won't like it.'

Jacques Offenbach, in his cheeky comic opera *Orpheus in the Underworld*, portrayed Jupiter and the gods as fed up with their life up there on Mount Olympus. For one thing, the catering is tedious, nectar and ambrosia and nothing else all day long. Life down there might be far more interesting, they conjecture, so they take a trip to the nether regions, going down in a lift in some stage productions, and there it turns out to be a riot of fun.

As Advent takes us joyfully into Christmas, I do not doubt that the Creator intended earth to be a pleasant garden suburb of heaven, not the barren outpost of hell that man in his madness and wickedness has often made it. So, let's not be troubled but thankful for this world God has made and loves, in which we make our home for a time, and where he chose to be 'earthed' for us and for our salvation.

5

I like Luke

Many a doctor, I mean of the medical kind, has been a writer too. Luke, almost certainly the author of the two-volume work, his *Gospel* and *The Acts of the Apostles*, was among the earliest. His special day in the church calendar is 18 October.

Clues to his basic profession may be spotted in the Gospel bearing his name. When he records the saying about rich men, camels and needles, he uses the Greek for a *surgeon's* needle (18: 25), whereas Matthew and Mark have the word for an ordinary domestic type (19: 24, 10: 25). Again, the first two Evangelists make no mention of Jesus 'sweating blood' in Gethsemane, but Luke does (22: 44). Was it because, as a medic, he was particularly aware of this clinical evidence for extreme anguish and fear? Such clues make the words of Luke exciting to read.

In the sequel to his Gospel, there are clear signs that, as a journalist, he accompanied Paul on the latter two of the Apostle's three missionary tours. In his *alter ego* as a writer Luke emerges as an eyewitness in passages where he writes 'we' rather than 'they' (eg Acts 16: 6-15). He was held in custody with Paul in Rome (2 Timothy 4: 11). He was freed; and one tradition says that he was a lifelong bachelor living on into his seventies or eighties in Bithynia (today's northern Turkey, bordering the southern shores of the Black Sea).

Was he a painter too? Some Spanish cathedral has a picture of the Virgin Mary alleged to have been Luke's doing; and he is supposed to have painted Our Lady as she may be viewed in the Church of Santa Maria Maggiore on the Esquiline Hill in Rome, one of eighty churches in the Eternal City dedicated to the BVM. How authentic these claims are, who can tell? Luke is also the patron saint of artists as well as of doctors and surgeons. Dante Gabriel Rossetti bade us

Give honour unto Luke Evangelist
For he it was (the aged legends say)
Who first taught Art to fold her hands and pray

I like 'our dear doctor', 'the beloved physician' (Colossians 4: 14)

I like Luke for *his literary prowess.*

His style is superior to anything else in the New Testament. He wrote for an educated Greek world, a Bernard Levin among hacks. He supplied both his works with a preface addressed to Theophilus. This is the hallmark of literary practice, and Luke alone among the New Testament writers follows it. The experts agree that the opening paragraph of *The Gospel according to Luke* is a fine example of Greek writing. A E Harvey, in his *Companion to the New Testament*, describes its author as 'a conscious literary stylist (this opening paragraph is a smooth and polished piece of Greek prose), ready to make use of the conventions of the world of letters'.

Who was Theophilus? I have often wondered. One theory is that Luke had been a slave who gained his freedom, and that Theophilus had been his master.

It was Doctor Luke, we believe, who wrote 'the loveliest story in the world', George Eliot's evaluation of the account of the Walk to Emmaus (Luke 24: 13-35). 'The story, you know,' enthused Malcolm Muggeridge in *Jesus Rediscovered*, 'is so incredibly vivid that no one who has ever tried to write can doubt it's authenticity.' Was Luke himself, as some believe, the unnamed companion of Cleopas on the homeward road to Emmaus? If so, then we have here another eyewitness account.

It was Luke who 'scooped' fifteen of the finest parables of Jesus. He alone gave us the Good Samaritan, the Prodigal, the Rich Fool, the Rich Man and Lazarus – to name a few of Doctor Luke's peerless 'exclusives'. To what degree, one speculates, do they owe their brilliance to Jesus himself or, in the manner of their literary preservation, to 'the beloved physician'?

I like Luke for his *devotional Gospel.*

It resounds with worship. Praise and prayer are its punctuation marks. Nowhere in the four Gospels do we catch Jesus praying more than in Luke. He prayed while being baptised in the Jordan, but only Luke tells us so (3: 21). He prayed the whole night through before choosing the special Twelve, but Luke alone mentions it (6: 12). 'But I have prayed for you, Simon,' said Jesus to Peter, predicting his denial, 'that your faith will not fail,' (22: 32). This, too, is exclusive to Luke, and further examples could be cited.

As for songs of celebratory praise, 'our dear doctor' claims them all – Magnificat, Benedictus, Nunc Dimittis. His first two chapters break into solo and choral hymns every few minutes, the Christmas chorale of angels making the Saviour's birth night anything but silent. Luke's version of the Christ Event ends with the disciples worshipping their Ascendant Master and returning to the city full of joy to spend their time of waiting for the Holy Spirit in worship (24: 52-53). 'Where others see but the dawn coming over the hill,' enthused William Blake, 'I see the soul of God shouting for joy.' Luke would have said amen to that.

I like Luke for *his respect for women.*

Thanks not least to him, women get rather a good press in the Gospels, according to Karen Armstrong in her book *The Gospel According to Woman.* 'They are not seen as irrelevant impediments,' she declared. 'Some of Jesus' best friends were women.' Let it be said that Jesus inaugurated a new world order reversing old ideas which regarded man as the norm and woman as no more than 'a failed man'. The teaching of Jesus liberated women from domestic triviality giving them a place equal to men.

The narrative of his visit to the Bethany home with its resultant row between Martha and her sister Mary is exclusively in Luke (10: 38-42); and it illustrates the clash between the old attitudes towards women and the new. Martha got worked up not because she was left to do the chores single-handed but because Mary was flouting hard-set contemporary convention. Men only were supposed to be instructed by a rabbi while the women, as Ms Armstrong explained, were left to 'tiptoe around and make sure everybody is comfortable, while the men talk'.

Luke, author of "the women's Gospel", was, like Jesus, way ahead of his time. Christian leaders in the ensuing centuries were yet to write women off as no more than childbearing machines or freaks of nature, seriously questioning whether they were human and had souls.

I like Luke, finally, for *his world view.*

He wrote for the Gentiles beyond the narrow confines of Judaism. Jesus had, after all, left clear orders that the gospel must be imparted to the whole wide world. In his Gospel Luke makes no restriction on the kind of audience when he reports how Jesus sent his men out on their mission (9: 1-6 & 10: 1-20). Matthew, however, has Jesus tell his missioners not to preach to Gentiles or Samaritans (10: 5). Luke, unlike Matthew, was never obsessed with the notion that everything Jesus did had to be a detailed fulfilment of Jewish prophecy. Luke's Jesus was addressed as 'Master' not 'Rabbi'. His family tree of Jesus goes back to Adam, founder of the whole human race (3: 23-38), whereas Matthew starts with Abraham (1: 1-17). In *A Calendar of Saints,* James Bentley underlined the fact that 'whenever Jesus has dealings with, for example, Syrians, or praises a Roman centurion, Luke tells us about it. He shows us Jesus caring for the black sheep of society'.

In Glasgow one day, the devotional essayist from New Zealand, Rita Snowden, was chatting over a cup of tea with William Barclay, the popular expositor. 'If I had to choose to keep one book of the New Testament, and one book only,' he told her, 'the book I would choose would be Luke's Gospel, for in it I believe we have Jesus at his most beautiful, and the Gospel at its widest.'

What more need be said about 'our dear doctor' than that?

6

The cure for thoughtlessness

We watched the latest re-run on TV of the superb film version of My *Fair Lady*, the musical play based on Shaw's Pygmalion, the story of a professor of phonetics, Henry Higgins, who trains a common flower girl Eliza Doolittle to speak like a duchess and successfully passes her off as such at a grand embassy ball. Then he and his friend Colonel Pickering return to the professor's home in Wimpole Street, exhausted but triumphant. With Eliza hovering in the background, they both totally ignore her and make for bed. 'I think I shall turn in too,' says the Colonel to Higgins. 'Still, it's been a great occasion; a triumph for you. Goodnight.'

It's a classic theatrical demonstration of *the callousness of sheer thoughtlessness.* The men, full of self-congratulation, completely ignore poor Eliza, yet she was the belle of the ball. Higgins has done with her now, and takes the full credit for the success of the venture. He has no more use for her. Or has he? The play ends uneasily. There is no hint of any special relationship between the two, though the musical concludes with Eliza returning to Higgins, who had grown accustomed to her face, and fetching his slippers for him.

There is real-life thoughtlessness too. When Stephen Pix was a vicar of a North Yorkshire parish, he had to stay at home at Christmas coping with the extra services the season brings, while it was left to his wife Isobel to ferry their younger son Christopher several times to York Minster, 35 miles to the south, where he was a chorister. She enjoyed the Minster services, but while the choir was practising she had to wait outside in the car, slowly freezing to death. The cathedral clergy all lived in Minster Yard, but even on Christmas Day no one invited Isobel into a warm house or offered her any form of refreshment. 'This sprang from thoughtlessness, not malice,' she said kindly, 'but as a result we determined never knowingly to leave anyone out in the cold.'

The celebrated botanist David Bellamy recollects his childhood in his autobiography *Jolly Green Giant*. The family were Baptists belonging to a flourishing Baptist Church in Surrey. Baptisms by total immersion were regularly held, sometimes a dozen at a time, with special robes worn by the candidates, black for men white for women.

David's mother would take the robes and towels home to launder them, and she herself carried the heavy load to the bus a couple of hundred yards away with a walk of over a quarter of a mile at the end of the journey. The holy laundry heavily wet was then put through the mangle.

David wrote in his book that this was grossly unfair, while the deacons passed by heedlessly in their cars, some even in their Rolls Royces. 'It was this, I believe,' he wrote, 'that first stirred the campaigner in my soul and eventually made me forsake the Baptist Church.'

Thoughtlessness, mistakenly assessed as a trivial fault, can have more serious consequences. Whenever I am guilty of this hurtful form of social neglect (and I don't say 'if ever...') let me learn to be more unselfishly observant of the welfare of others, less obsessively preoccupied with the devices and desires of my own heart. And let me search the scriptures for a man named Ebed-Melech,

Hidden away in the obscurer pages of the Old Testament lies a very short story worthy of our attention (Jeremiah 38). Six centuries before Jesus came, Jeremiah the prophet like Joseph and the Amazing Technicolor Dreamcoat, was thrown into a pit. He had been preaching uncomfortable truths said to be bad for public morale, and some officials were determined to shut him up – literally. The pit would have been a well, an empty and muddy cistern. In this dank, bottle-shaped prison the prophet was left to die, either by starvation or perhaps rather sooner from suffocation. News of this cruelty reached a man employed in the royal household whose name was Ebed-Melech. He was a Cushite, an Ethiopian.

He hurried off to see the king and managed to get permission to rescue Jeremiah. 'Very well,' said the king, 'you'd better take three men with you and pull him out before he dies.' So Jeremiah was hauled out. But not just that. Ebed-Melech took extra trouble to do it in the gentlest and most thoughtful manner. On the way to the well, he and his assistants called in at the quartermaster's stores and requisitioned some old clothing. These cast-offs and remnants he let down with the ropes. 'He told me to put the rags under my arms,' said Jeremiah, recalling the experience, 'so that the ropes wouldn't hurt me. I did this, and they pulled me up out of the well.'

There was no thoughtlessness here. Looking down at Tintern Abbey, Wordsworth wrote that the 'best portion of a good man's life' consisted of 'his little, nameless, unremembered acts of kindness.' The cushioning ministry of Ebed-Melech the Cushite, however, has not been forgotten. 'Kindness,' stated Johann Wolfgang von Goethe, 'is the golden chain by which society is bound together.'

Let us now search the scriptures again, for a prescription for thoughtlessness. Its cure lies in five words in the third chapter of Ezekiel. He was both priest and prophet, and he had followed his people to their exile hundreds of miles away in Babylon. In the old translation he says: 'I sat where they sat.' In the Revised English Bible he adds: '... and for seven days I stayed there, overcome by what I had seen and heard.' He lived as a deportee for a week, getting alongside the exiles; and he was 'overwhelmed' and 'dumbfounded' say the versions. From direct experience he knew what it was like to be an exile.

In the archives of Christian mission there are many stories of pioneering evangelists who have followed Ezekiel's example, training themselves in the art of getting alongside those they had come to evangelize. John Woolman, missioner to the Indians, 'felt in his own body with his five senses what it was to live as a slave'. Vincent de Paul, the saint among the galley slaves, rowed sweating side by side with the rough, swearing men he so wanted to help and bring to Christ.

Much misunderstanding, even suffering, is the result of a thoughtlessness that fails, even refuses, to 'sit where they sit', to look at life through the eyes of the other fellow, to see it as he or she sees it. The poet Edwin Muir commended to his contemporaries what he termed the practice of *inseeing*. He imagined a dog standing nearby. He must try to understand the creature. He must strive to get inside that dog's head, to look out on the world from the dog's viewpoint. Then he would be better able to deal with the animal as a dog deserves.

Inseeing is an art to be cultivated at the purely human level too.

In days gone by at ordination and induction services, it was customary to include two 'Charges'; one to the Minister, the other to the Church. Sometimes, the two became one. If ever it fell to me to cover both in a single address, I would begin with those five words: 'I sat where they sat.' Let the minister sit where his people sit, and let the people stand where he stands. When preachers go to their pulpits, let them put themselves in the place of the congregation.

There is a sense in which no preachers worth their salt preach from the pulpit but from the pew. A wise pastor will try to see life from the congregation's angle, endeavouring to enter into their pains, sorrows, disappointments, frustrations. The church is the people, not a building or a burdensome package of problems. A leading educationalist once said to a group of teachers, 'Always remember, you are not teaching history, or geography, or mathematics; you are teaching John, and Harry, and Mary!' Bonhoeffer said: 'We must learn to regard people less in the light of what they do or omit to do, and more in the light of what they suffer.'

Conversely, let the congregation imaginatively stand where the minister stands. It takes some doing to prepare and deliver a sermon, to plan and conduct an act of worship. The process drains our nervous, emotional and physical energies. Kindness to your minister takes the form of your closest and disciplined attention and response, even if he is a bit of a bore. And let those who dwell in pews and nod off in them, or switch off, bear in mind that they may themselves be boring the poor old minister.

A dear old lady in one of my pastorates lived in a small house in which she always kept the front room steamily hot. This, the gas up high, plus her prattling on and on, nearly put me to sleep in the armchair one November afternoon. My predecessor, she told me in disgust, actually dropped off to sleep while visiting her one day. Some pastoral calls can be simply boring, especially if the person concerned insists on talking each time at length about their ailments. Put yourself in your minister's place, I say. Sit where he or she sits, and see if you don't nod off!

7

The preacher with a pen

In my callow youth I felt I should attempt to preach a sermon. My childhood sweetheart said cautiously, 'Try it and see.' This I did, as part of a youth team, at Theale in Berkshire one quiet autumn evening in 1946. I 'tried it and saw' at several other out-of-town Congregational chapels during the following months.

Growing speedily aware of my abundant ignorance in matters of theology and religion, I turned for help and inspiration to my minister, the Revd Aubrey Vine, then about to become a Doctor of Divinity and I soon to be his son-in-law. He allowed me to browse among the many books in his study. Through the wartime years, I had listened intently to his preaching. I had noted especially his regular use of illustrations and quotations to liven and light up his themes. As might be expected, I was drawn to the homiletical section of his library, where volumes of sermons and books about the art and craft of preaching were to be found.

It was there that I discovered a book with the arresting title *The Luggage of Life*, by an author named F W Boreham. I found it contained 32 devotional essays with intriguing titles like 'Mad Dogs and Mosquitoes', 'Our Rubbish Heaps', 'On the Wisdom of Conducting One's Own Funeral' and 'Hat-Pins and Button-Hooks.' There were other books like it on those shelves, and I asked their owner about them and their author. 'Boreham,' he said, 'Is most useful for ideas and illustrations for sermons.' So that's where he gets them from, I thought. Well, some of them anyway. From then onwards through the years, I have collected over forty Borehams and accumulated a heap of gratitude to both Boreham and Vine for the help they have given me in providing ideas, illustrations and the apt quotation for my sermons too. I bought my own copy of *The Luggage of Life* from a second-hand bookseller in July 1947.

Who was Frank W Boreham? An Australian minister? It seemed so, for in a brief preface to that book, the author wrote: 'These leaves are of Australian growth.' Further, that preface told me that he was writing from Hobart, Tasmania, July 1912. He was English, in fact Kentish.

Young Boreham, twenty-four years of age and trained for the Baptist ministry at Spurgeon's College, accepted an invitation to a pastorate in faraway Australia at Mosgiel, a small township of a thousand or so inhabitants. He left behind his family and Stella, with whom he had fallen in love, but she soon followed him and they were married.

It was at Mosgiel that he began to blossom out as a writer. At home in his 'teens in the 1880s, he had managed to get into print through newspapers. Now he persuaded the editor of a modest twice-weekly publication to give him space. Each Saturday he contributed a sermon from his own pulpit. Later, he became editor of the *New Zealand Baptist* and wrote its editorials for ten years. Thus began a writing career which continued for the rest of his days.

Boreham would be seated in his study at eight every morning, ready to begin. All his writing throughout his long life was done with a pen in flowing calligraphy. He scorned the typewriter, though I suspect that he would have been willing to try a word-processor, if only such a device had been available in his day. Its sub-editing facilities would have saved him hours of recopying. But no typewriters in his household, nor a telephone to interrupt his work, until the later years.

After twelve years at Mosgiel, Frank and Stella Boreham moved to Hobart in Tasmania where they spent ten years before moving to Armadale, a suburb of Melbourne. There he wrote regularly for mainland journals in Sydney and Melbourne. His fellow-ministers urged him to seek a publisher for his writings to preserve them in book form. The outcome was that in July 1912 *The Luggage of Life* was published. My copy was part of the tenth edition which appeared in May 1921. So began the literary career of a best-selling international author,

To say he wrote prolifically is to put it far too mildly. Indeed, he wrote frantically, and for a reason. J T Soundy was a staunch and trusted friend at Hobart. They happened to be travelling in the train one day when Mr Soundy suddenly asked him how old he was. Thirty-six, came the reply. 'Take my advice,' said the old man gravely. 'Make the most of it. You'll have very few fresh ideas after you're forty.' This alarmed Boreham. It galvanized him into writing and writing, not hurriedly but steadily. He sent off manuscripts needed for immediate publication and packed the surplus in boxes. Whenever he went away on holiday, he packed those packages of manuscripts in watertight coverings and buried them safe from fire and flood in the garden.

After producing thirty volumes in a quarter of a century, he claimed to have written his last in 1936 when he was sixty-five years of age. His publishers urged him to continue, and he did. To the joy of his readership, out came twenty-seven more sparkling essays under the title *I Forgot to Say*, and the books kept appearing until he died in 1959. His final volume was entitled *The Last Mile*.

Near the end of his days and just before his son drove him to the Royal Melbourne Hospital, the old man handed him a bundle of articles enough to fill the papers for months.

My enthusiasm for the writings of F W Boreham led me to produce a collection of thirty-one essays in the Boreham style under the title *A Month of Sundays in 1964*. It was well received and pleasingly reviewed. Erik Routley wrote flatteringly in *The British Weekly* and commended the book heartily, and he wrote to me personally. The *Irish Christian Advocate* stated that I wasn't merely an echo of Boreham but 'a new springing of the root' of Borehamism. Not, I should quickly add, that I was consciously imitating him. I never felt competent to do so.

There is this, however, to amuse. In April 1969, I received a letter from Mr S Jones of Impington, Cambridge, addressed to the 'Revd F W Boreham, Minister of Winton Congregational Church, Bournemouth.' By then I had left Bournemouth, but it reached me. Mr Jones wanted to know if I had any more Borehamesque books available for him. He had read my second volume *A Handful of Minutes* as well as the first. But the 1960s saw a breakdown in religious publishing, and devotional and other such books suddenly became much more expensive. Good churchgoing folk wouldn't spend the money on them. Otherwise, I might have written more of the same.

Returning to the Borehams, I read that theirs was a happy marriage, their story a love story. They had produced a family of five, four of them girls. Dr Irving Benson of Wesley Church, Melbourne, said of Frank Boreham: 'A quiet insight, a gentle humour, a homely philosophy and a charming literary grace, but supremely he was a man with a message.' Defining his intended aim, the man himself said: 'I want to scatter benedictions as thickly as autumn leaves,' Of his writing career he once joked, 'If there is anything in the doctrine of reincarnation, I intend to spend at least one of my future spans of existence as a novelist.'

In his eighty-eighth year, he was serene, still mentally alert if otherwise frail, and full of honours. A few months before he died, Australia was visited by Billy Graham. He let it be known that the one person he was keen to meet was Dr F W Boreham, and so it came to pass. 'Before we left,' wrote Irving Benson, 'I asked the dear old Doctor to bless us, and there Billy Graham and I knelt, while with his face uplifted to Heaven and his hands on our heads, he poured out his great heart in a prayer which will follow us through the years like the sound of a great Amen.'

There is a strange, almost eerie, postscript. One sunny afternoon in Tunbridge Wells when Frank was a baby in his pram, his nurse took him for a walk. While she was resting on a wayside seat, along came a gipsy caravan. Trudging beside the leading vehicle was an old crone wrinkled with age, bent nearly double and limping on two sticks. Spotting the pram, she came over and looked at the baby's face. She took the baby's hand in hers. Turned it over and examined it thoughtfully. After a brief silence, she said huskily to the nurse: 'Tell his mother to put a pen in his hand and he'll never want for a living.' And away she went.

8

A merry Christmas?

The word 'merry' overused during the Christmas season, poses problems for senior chapel people.   In popular parlance it suggests drunkenness; and one doesn't need to be a narrow-minded, killjoy Puritan to deplore that.

Jokes galore have been made about being the worse for drink. W C Fields, the old-time film actor, poured out an endless stream of them. 'A woman drove me to drink,' he more than once said, 'and I never even had the courtesy to thank her.' Witty perhaps, but not funny when you consider what excessive drinking does to people, and more important to those around them,

So, if 'merry' means drunk, should we wish each other that kind of Christmas? What a way to honour the birth of the Saviour! 'One reason I don't drink,' said Nancy Astor, 'is that I want to know when I am having a good time.' Quite. Not that to have a drink necessarily means to get drunk, except in the sorry case of the alcoholic for whom the first and not the one over the eight does the harm. There is nothing 'merry' about a drunk.

I have been researching the word. It occurs about thirty times in the Authorized Version. In almost all cases, it doesn't mean to be drunk. I can find only one clear instance where, at any rate in the Good News Bible, it seems to. In Genesis, when Joseph in Egypt received his brothers, he treated them generously; and the old Bible tells us that 'they drank, and were merry with him'. Only in the Good News, so far as I can make out, does it explicitly say, 'They ate and drank with Joseph until they were drunk' (Genesis 43: 34). Otherwise, 'merry' is translated as joyful, happy, jovial, cheerful.

The word originally had nothing to do with inebriation or even with what the temperance advocates called 'strong drink'. It simply meant 'lively, active', even 'famous'. Hence 'Merrie England', which doesn't mean that the populace were all staggering about 'stoned out of their minds', as the saying goes. Robin Hood's 'Merry Men' were, we suppose, a lively but not a drunken lot, otherwise how could they have shot a straight arrow? A merry-go-round is a fairground device not a pub crawl. At Christmas we sing of the 'merry organ', suggesting not that it is 'well-oiled' but playing bright sprightly music. Furthermore, be careful where you put the comma when you sing the eighteenth-century carol 'God rest you merry, gentlemen'. It comes after not before our word. It isn't a prayer that God may enable us to sleep it off. It means 'May God keep you joyful'.

Our word crops up four times in the King James Bible's narrative of the Parable of the Prodigal Son in Luke chapter 15. For example, when the wayward son comes home, a feast was quickly organized; and it says in verse 24, 'And they began to be merry.' Now, if our preachers consult the varied versions of that verse, three of them at least will provide the wherewithal for a sermon.

'And they began to be merry.' In the Good News Bible it says: 'And so the feasting began.'

A merry Christmas involves extra eating and drinking for most of us. We 'feast'.

When I was a boy, a girl named Rita lived next door. A large girl she was, a younger sister she could have been to Friar Tuck. Every Christmas without fail she tucked into the goodies and was invariably too ill to welcome the new year a week later. The silly girl gluttonized, as many do. Feasting and gluttony are two different things; like drinking and drunkenness. Jesus feasted. He attended dinner parties. He went for the company more than the food, it seems. Yet he surely enjoyed the food.

Monica Furlong was a perceptive writer on spirituality, and in her book *Christian Uncertainties* she distinguished between feasting and gluttony. Feasting, she insisted, is a delight marked by gratitude, gaiety and humour, by an awareness of pleasure and an overflowing love. 'We are rich' she wrote, 'God, you might say, is present.' Greed, on the other hand, is earnest and anxious. The emphasis lies not on the delight of tasting but on 'getting' the food or drink inside you. 'There is something solitary and guilty about the compulsion,' she concluded.

Let us never feel guilty about feasting in the right way because so many in this unjust world starve. So long, that is, as we play some part in their relief

Eight-hundred years ago, Saint Hugh was Bishop of Lincoln. Attributed to him are these words: 'Eat well and drink well, and serve God well and devoutly.' He was known and revered for his liberality to the poor and lepers; but clearly he was no guilty killjoy when it came to the good things of life. 'Go ahead,' it says in Ecclesiastes, '... eat your food and be happy, drink your wine and be cheerful. It's all right with God' (9: 7). 'And they began to be merry.' In the Revised English Bible it says: 'And the *festivities* began.'

The American theologian Harvey Cox reminded us that we are creatures who not only work and think but who sing, dance, pray, tell stories and celebrate. This is *homo festivus*.

What is known as the Protestant work-ethic has taught us to look upon work as all-important. These other things must be regarded as a secondary, sudsidiary activity of humankind. Martin Luther set us going along this path, and Karl Marx reinforced the notion. Hence, good chapelgoers have been known to tut-tut when firms and businesses shut down for a ten-day Christmas. Scrooge wanted Bob Cratchit to work on Christmas Day itself.

What is the chief end of man?' asks *The Shorter Catechism*. To work? No. It is 'to glorify God and enjoy him for ever'. This, of course, includes work in which we are meant to find creative fulfilment despite its chores and burdens. But let's note, God and enjoyment go together. Festivity is closely linked with religion. Somewhere the Old Testament says: 'They all went into their vineyards and picked the grapes, made wine from them and held a festival.' The old Bible continues by saying that they 'made merry, and went into the house of their god, and did eat and drink'. It was Democritus, centuries before Christ, who said: 'The life without festival is a long road without an inn.' So then, a merry Christmas!

'And they began to be merry.' The Jerusalem Bible says: 'And they began to *celebrate.*'

Christians have the best reasons for celebrating. In his *Marmion* Sir Waiter Scott wrote that England was merry England at Christmas time. ' 'Twas Christmas told the merriest tale,' he declared. Old Dr Johnson in March 1781 said, according to Boswell, 'This merriment of parsons is mighty offensive.' To what he was referring we don't know. Old King Canute, a thousand years ago, described the monks at Ely as merrily singing. Their faith gave them every cause for such celebration.

Some years ago during our sojourn in the Cotswolds, we called on Laurie Lee, still living at the time in his home village of Slad, to record something for my radio programme to be broadcast across Gloucestershire on Christmas morning. He got lyrical, as often he did, over the carol singing of his boyhood in Slad, so movingly recounted in *Cider with Rosie.* I was there to tape an interview with him, which we did; but he asked if he might read a passage from the book. With difficulty and through a magnifying glass, his sight failing, he read it. Then he reiterated what Pete Seeger had put into one of his own songs. Why can't we have Christmas all the year round?

I reminded Laurie that the Church celebrates Easter every Sunday because it's the Resurrection not the Birth that is ultimately of more significance for us. Christmas rightly comes but once a year. Part of its appeal is just that; and calendars mark the day in red. Another American scholar, Josef Pieper remarked that 'the festive quality of a holiday depends on its being exceptional'. Like all celebrations.

So then, a merry Christmas!

9

The comfort of the stars

Lovers of poetry will readily recall *Sea Fever,* John Masefield's nostalgic mood poem. In addition to 'the wheel's kick and the wind's song and the white sail's shaking', not to mention 'a grey mist on the sea's face and a grey dawn breaking', the poet in his reverie says, 'and all I ask is a tall ship and *a star to steer her by*'. But what does one do if the star to steer by isn't there? What if it and its twinkling brothers and sisters in the sky have been totally blotted out by black storm and impenetrable cloud?

Nowadays, the sophisticated devices of modern technology enable seamen to dispose of that anxiety before they embark. The ocean navigator need no longer depend on the stars.

Paul of Tarsus and his fellow-voyagers, crossing a rough and unpredictable Mediterranean long before radio and radar and rescue services were on hand, were directly dependent upon those fixed and reliable stars up there. It was, therefore, a terrifying prospect if, as the narrative in Acts 27 tells us: 'For days on end there was no sign of either sun or stars.' That's exactly as it was on that long, adventurous trip to Rome. Vivid is the narrative, written by eyewitness Luke.

The comfort of the stars. Ancient man found their permanence and sheer reliability a source of confidence and reassurance as he moved about his world, not least on the shifting, uncertain sea. Imagine him, far out on the waters and a long way from land, looking up at the clear night sky and finding comfort in identifying the Plough, the Pointers, the Pole Star. The sight of these anchored him in a sense to the land he had left, for these could be seen from terra firma too. Caesar, in Shakespeare's play, says: 'But I am constant as the northern star, of whose true fixed and resting quality there is no fellow in the firmament.'

The lifelong preacher thinks in threes. I apply this principle to the stars.

To begin with, they bear a *geographical* significance.

My early literary inspiration Frank Boreham, recorded in one of his charming essays what happened when he reached the End of the World. Such was the name of a remote Australian sheep station he was visiting. The next-door neighbours were 20 miles away. It was creepily quiet at dusk when he and his companions reached their destination after a tiring, dusty journey.

After a meal and a long chat in front of a huge log-fire, Boreham stepped out on to the verandah to take a look at the night. The stars were in their finest form, galaxies of them, it seemed. He was entranced. He strolled to the gate to get a better view.

There he met a young governess named Grace. She too was gazing at the bright, clear night sky, her elbows resting on the gate. She turned as he approached.

'I always come out here on a night like this,' she said. 'It does me good and cures my homesickness.' She explained that her home was in Melbourne. She was a city girl. But a governess was needed at the End of the World, and the pay was attractive to someone like her in need of the money.

'But, oh, it's so different from Melbourne in the daytime,' she went on, 'and home seems an eternity away. But at night this gate seems just like the gate at home. And the stars come out, the very same stars that I used to watch from our dear old front garden. It is lovely to see them. They seem so companionable, and when I stand here and look at them I forget that I am at the End of the World. I sometimes think I could never stay here but for them!'

Many of us could, I am sure, recall a similar experience of our own. Mine takes me back to my two years of National Service, and to a night of guard duty on the edge of a wood above those bonnie bonnie banks of Loch Lomond. I felt homesick as I clearly remember, these sixty years on. Yet it helped to look up at the sharply focused autumn sky. Those same comforting stars, I knew, were looking down upon my loved ones more than four hundred miles southward.

The stars also bear a *historical* significance.

Come to think of it, the distance between places isn't the only kind to be bridged by the stars. They span the years and the centuries. They look down upon the procession of history, and as we gaze up at them, we are linked in an exciting way with our ancestors back down the long corridor of the ages. Standing in our garden on a clear night have we never been enthralled by such a thought? Dull would anyone be who hasn't and empty are those who shrug the shoulder apathetically at such a question. Edward Shillito wrote verses on this very theme. The heavens upon whose wealth of wonder the city sophisticate yawns with stolid indifference are, he wrote,

> *The heavens, beneath which Alfred stood, when he*
> > *Built ramparts by the tide against his foes*
> *The skies men loved when in eternity;*
> > *The dream-like Abbey rose;*

> *The heavens whose glory has not known increase*
> > *Since Raleigh swaggered home by lantern-light,*
> *And Shakespeare, looking upwards, knew the peace,*
> > *The cool deep peace of night.*

> *Under those heavens brave Wesley rose betimes*
> > *To preach ere daybreak to the tender soul,*
> *And in the heart of Keats the starry rhymes*
> > *Roll, and for ever roll*

So then, the stars link us with our ancestors. They remind us of 'the communion of saints'. The Church Militant upon earth now is bound up together with the Church Triumphant in heaven, the fellowship of Christians from yesterday and all the yesterdays before it. Go outside tonight, weather permitting and clouds allowing, and stop, look up and think on these things.

Or, if you will, pay a visit to the London Planetarium. I haven't been able to get there, I confess, for a long time. But I managed to do so some years ago. By means of a complicated electronic instrument in a historico-astronomical lecture, they showed us the night-sky as it would have been in the varying ages gone by. That place I felt at the time was a temple, and a lecture there isn't merely educational entertainment. It can be a spiritual experience. It isn't surprising that Patrick Moore bears a permanently amazed expression on his countenance. Anyone whose life and work entails constant looking up at the stars in the sky through telescopes must live in a constant state of wonder, and it is bound to show on the face. The stars bridge the events of history as we view them outside in the garden or on a screen in some astronomer's temple.

Last of all, the stars bear a *religious* significance.

I have heard tell of an old man who had been born at the start of the nineteenth century. He was bent nearly double and tottered about leaning heavily on a pair of sticks. He sat outside his back door in the evenings, smoking a churchwarden's long pipe. Children gathered round him. They were overawed and fascinated. He told them of what he remembered seeing when he was their age and younger. There were the first railway trains ever. He had heard William Pitt speak. His elder brother had fought under the mighty Duke of Wellington. One evening, all the children had slipped away except one who stayed on, spellbound. He helped the old man light his pipe. There was a long silence. The lad then quietly made a move to rejoin the others. The old man, however, restrained him, laying a hand on his head. Looking at him full in the face, he said: 'My boy, if you live to be as old as I am, you will learn that there are only two sets of things in life. There are the things that change, and they are very wonderful. And there are the things that never change, and they are more wonderful still.' The boy in question never forgot that moment of revelation. It was almost the last thing the old man said.

'Lift up your eyes to the heavens,' cried Isaiah, 'consider who created it all, led out their host one by one and called them all by their names.' All that time ago, he too was directing people's gaze to the comfort of the stars (40: 26). And looking upward, we see Jesus, described on the Bible's final page as 'the bright star of dawn', – the unchanging Jesus Christ Superstar who shines upon our world eternally, and whose brightness will never be put out.

10

Did Jesus need to be baptised?

The season of Epiphany is a busy time in the church calendar. Several themes present themselves. Twelfth Night marks the end of the Christmas festivities when customs originating in the pagan world were honoured. One such was the appointment of a child to be king. It was a time for merrymaking and Shakespeare's *Twelfth Night* was meant to be performed as part of the revels. The actual feast of Epiphany falls on the sixth of January when, in the Book of Common Prayer, we are exhorted to acknowledge 'the manifestation of Christ to the Gentiles' by the showing of the infant Jesus to the Magi. Strictly, this is the day when the Wise Men make their entry into the drama of the Nativity. They were never at the crib, but it is convenient to find them a place there in church and school nativity plays, where they crowd the stable alongside the shepherds for the group photos and the camcorder recordings.

Epiphany points us to the first miracle Jesus performed as he attended the wedding reception in Cana, turning water into wine. It is also the time to dwell on his baptism in the Jordan.

We cannot dodge a difficult question. *Did Jesus need to be baptised?*

Baptisms by John in the Jordan were cleansing rituals of repentance for the remission of sins. How could they possibly apply to the Christ? John was obviously taken aback when Jesus came to him with the request. He tried to make Jesus change his mind, but John agreed to do it (Matthew 3: 13-17).

Did Jesus submit to baptism to please his mother Mary and his brothers? An absurd question, you might say. But so says *The Gospel according to the Hebrews*, an ancient document supposed to be a sort of first draft of the Gospel of Matthew. Any minister will tell you that some mothers bring their babies to be baptised under pressure from grandparents.

A more important question is why Jesus wanted to be baptised. Was it, we wonder, meant to represent *a precise time and place for the launch of his ministry?*

Here we jump from the sixth of January to the sixth of June. On that day in 1944 more than four thousand ships embarked from our shores to cross the Channel for the invasion of Europe. It was D-Day, the day of decision and of destiny. Jesus had his own D-Day. It came after nearly twenty years of working in the family business in Nazereth where 'silent at Joseph's side he stood, and smoothed and trimmed the shapeless wood'. The D-Day of Jesus was his own baptism. It was there on the riverbank as he stepped out of the water that the gentle but irresistible invasion of God's love into the hearts of humankind began in a new way. It was then that Jesus made his resolve to enter upon the mission to which he had been called, and for which he was uniquely equipped from above.

Many lives seem to lack any resolve. The eighteenth-century parson-poet Edward Young, in his long poem *Night Thoughts* admirably encapsulates the undisciplined life.

> *At thirty man suspects himself a fool;*
> *Knows it at forty, and reforms his plan;*
> *At fifty chides his infamous delay,*
> *Pushes his prudent purpose to resolve;*
> *In all the magnanimity of thought*
> *Resolves; and re-resolves; then dies the same.*

The nearest most of us come to resolve is when the New Year Resolutions are made; but then they are generally so trivial and last so briefly, often broken like a child's cheap Christmas toy by about the fifth of January.

Without doubt the lives of those who contribute best to the life of humanity, even in small and provincial ways, are marked by some hour of decision, some moment of solemn resolve, some D-Day which can be precisely chronicled. Without such a thing somewhere along the line, Homo Sapiens lives a discontented life because it is undirected. We resemble swamps rather than rivers, dissipated and going nowhere instead of following a set and purposeful course. The poet John Oxenham wrote:

> To every man there openeth
> A way and ways and a way;
> The high soul treads the high way,
> And the low soul gropes the low,
> And in between on the misty flats,
> The rest drift to and fro.

There was no drifting for Jesus. He was baptised; and the very word, certainly in its past tense, actually means to be 'submerged'. Whether he was physically dipped beneath the waters of Jordan (a mucky river) is doubtful. It is more likely that John stood beside him, the water waist high, and poured it over the sacred head destined to be sore wounded as a consequence of that resolve. Yet, so far as the commitment Jesus made goes, he went right in, sunk himself in it, gave himself totally.

When James and John, the ambitious sons of Zebedee, asked for privileged places in the coming kingdom, Jesus said reprovingly to them: 'Can you be baptised in the way I must be baptised?' Were they ready to be submerged in the waters of hate and hostility, of rejection and seeming failure, of suffering and finally of a cruel death? Such was the cost of the resolve Jesus made in the waters of the Jordan that day, that D-Day. C S Lewis once remarked: 'If you want a religion to make you feel really comfortable, I certainly don't recommend Christianity.'

Christian baptism should never be regarded as a religious rite of little or no relevance to the living of life in the world of today. Jesus himself obviously recognised its supreme importance for himself and for his followers. The two sacraments honoured in Protestant Reformed Christianity are Baptism and the Lord's Supper. Of the latter the risen Lord says, 'Do this in remembrance of me.' This obligation may be applied also to the former.

During 1987, Andrew Wilson wrote a series of reports in a national newspaper based on a visit to the Soviet Union. In the last of his articles he dealt with religious faith in Russia. 'Forget about Glasnost,' he cried excitedly. 'I have witnessed a Resurrection in the midst of an atheist State that is nothing short of a miracle.' He reported on the churches he had seen, filled as they were with a new generation of intelligent young people. 'This is no mere survival or curiosity, ' he stressed. 'It is unstoppable Resurrection ... In the West, where we have devoted ourselves so completely to the service of Mammon, the Christian religion has all but died. In the land where Lenin tried to abolish both God and Mammon religion prospers as never before.' He quoted the prophecy of Dostoevsky of 140 years ago to the effect that if Christianity survived in the world, it would not be because of Rome nor of Canterbury but because of Russia.

Reading A N Wilson's report, I found elsewhere in my archives what Moscow radio had said in March 1963 about Christian baptism. It was, believe it or not, condemned as a 'health menace', almost like AIDS today, and as 'a senseless and dangerous rite'. In the weekly pro-atheist broadcast, the Communist spokesman said that 'thousands' of babies died of pneumonia following christening ceremonies and that 'weak hearts' and 'weak lungs' in adults had been traced to baptisms in their early years. Baptism, it was claimed, kept the average life expectancy to 32 years during the time of the Czars because in those days every Russian was baptised. During the Communist years, however, government health services together with a considerable reduction in baptisms had, it was stated, increased life expectancy to 69 years.

These absurdities arose because the Soviet authorities saw baptism as bearing about it something of profound and alarming and revolutionary significance. They saw it as containing a deep and abiding power inimical to their atheistic purposes, for here was a life-transforming ceremony, a means of dedication to that Great Mystery which Andrew Wilson sensed when he shared in the worship of the Russian Orthodox one Sunday during his visit to Russia.

St Louis of France used to sign his documents not 'Louis IX, King but Louis of Poissy'. Asked why, he replied: 'Poissy is the place where I was baptised. I think more of the place where I was baptised than of Rheims Cathedral where I was crowned. It is a greater thing to be a child of God than to be the ruler of a Kingdom: this last I shall lose at death, but the other will be my passport to everlasting glory.'

11

Amen to that, brother!

I had an ebullient colleague in the ministry who had a habit of saying, 'Amen to that, brother. ' He could easily be switched on. If I said, 'There's nothing quite like a large bowl of porridge on a frosty, wintry morning,' he would be sure to trot out, 'Amen to that, brother!' Or, if I said, 'I always sink into the armchair and put my feet up on a Sunday evening after a busy day's preaching' his Pavlovian reflexes would be activated instantly with an 'Ay-men to that, brother!'

Amen crops up at various points in every act of worship. It means 'so be it', – 'may it be as has been asked, said or promised.' It is our response to the sentiments expressed in hymn, prayer, reading, or blessing. It comes from the Hebrew adjective meaning, firm, true, steadfast. In our use of the word, it is an adverb – truly, truly. When Jesus said, 'Truly, truly, I say to you,' he was using the Greek word amen, amen. We Christians have taken it, as we have taken much else, from synagogue worship. It appears again and again in both Testaments. No word is more liturgically familiar to us.

In the strange book of Revelation, Jesus Christ is portrayed as the Amen. That is, the True One whose words and promises are sure and certain. Those who first heard the message of John the Divine in Revelation needed this reassurance. The book was written in code, we are told, to the first-century underground church under pressure of persecution. Still, today, the towering truth that Jesus Christ is the Amen is an enormous strength and comfort to us, especially in loss, sorrow, illness and disappointment.

Jesus Christ, the Amen. Let me take you along a line of thought arising from this picture.

Jesus Christ, the Amen – the Test of Fitness.

If he is the supreme test of an idea, a word, a deed, a way of living, we may ask ourselves, 'Can we honestly say to this or to that, … "through Jesus Christ, our Lord, Amen"?'

All drivers should know that it is illegal to drive on incorrectly inflated tyres. For an offence of this kind a driver can be prosecuted, have his licence endorsed and be subject to a heavy fine. What is more, he can be caught out if he relies on the pressure gauges to be found on filling station forecourts. The AA warns us that they can be notoriously inaccurate. Some time ago, the Government completed a three-year survey of 48,000 forecourt tyre-pressure gauges. Eleven per cent were seriously inaccurate, while another seven per cent were found to be dangerously so. The Weights and Measures inspectors visit forecourts regularly for spot checks. One imagines an official arriving for a check with the accurate standard testing gauge against which the local one is to be tested for fitness.

So, the ideas we entertain, the values we embrace, and the ways and habits of the society around us are all subject to a fitness test against the standard of Christ. A solemn thought is this. Any who set out on life as committed followers of such a Lord and Master will know clearly to what they can and cannot say Amen. He is the supreme Test of Fitness.

Next, Jesus Christ, the Amen – the Seal of Approval.

Baptised by John in the Jordan, he became sure of his authority as he emerged from the river. The stamp of divine approval lay in the words: 'You are my beloved Son; in you I take delight.' (Luke 3: 22) Later, on the mountain of transfiguration, the voice from the cloud said: 'This is my own dear Son – listen to him!' (Mark 9: 7) He had the power of the Spirit with him. On he went to preach, teach and heal, till he reached the Cross and died and triumphed over death. His Father God had said Amen to him, and to the ministry he now faced.

Does the risen Lord say Amen to us? Can we claim his approval of all we say and do?

The tale is told of a boy of ten on holiday in London. His doting aunt couldn't think what to do with him to keep him amused. She finally decided that the best option was the British Museum. Plenty there to engage his lively mind for several days. So she sent him off to that erudite establishment with a packet of sandwiches each morning. It seems, however, that you can have too much even of a good thing. When the poor lad retired to bed at night, he would lie there in the dark, cowering. For it seemed that the mighty Assyrian gods were gazing threateningly down upon him, and the creepy Egyptian mummies were crawling all over his eiderdown. Suddenly one night he sat up and said to them loudly, 'I wonder what Jesus would make of you lot. ' Then he turned over and dropped peacefully into sleep, his morbid fears finally banished.

We may well ask ourselves what Jesus would make of us. Would we merit his Amen, could we claim his approval? Uncomfortable questions, I grant you.

Last of all, Jesus Christ the Amen – the Last Word.

King Shedad of Irem, says the story, built a wonderful palace. It was an impressive edifice containing everything a man could desire, and more elegant than any mind could envisage. 'Hast thou ever seen such a sight as this?' he said proudly to the prophet Houd. 'Canst thou tell the value of these things?' The prophet replied: 'Only in the hour of death can a man value such things.' It was a typical guru-type reply, and it annoyed the king. 'Hast thou fault to find with this building?' he burst out indignantly. 'Yea, the walls are weak,' answered Houd. 'They cannot keep out the angel of death.'

It was a chilling and deflating reminder that death is the great leveller. It is the universal experience with which all people without exception must come to terms sooner or later. In the face of death, nothing appears on the surface to be of any value, nor does anything seem worthwhile. Death stalks abroad among humankind as the last word on life.

Is it? Not when we are confronted by the Christ. Just as Amen is the last word in our prayers and services, so is he in our earthly life. He teaches us that death isn't the final catastrophe. There are worse things that can happen to us. Jesus insisted that those who can kill the body have no more that they can do, and so we need not fear them. Not to be afraid for this reason at the point of death is possibly the most demanding thing Jesus says to us. The truth is that he himself, not 'the Grim Reaper', has the last word. He is the Alpha and Omega, the first and the last, the Author and Finisher the Lord of life and death.

The early Christian community seems to have displayed unusual courage over the prospect of death. It was said that the followers of this Jesus during those early days out-thought outlived and *out-died* their contemporaries. 'What is death at most?' said St John Chrysostom in the fourth century. 'It is a journey for a season: a sleep longer than usual. If thou fearest death, thou shouldst also fear sleep.' St Athanasius, a contemporary, commented that 'Man is by nature afraid of death and of the dissolution of the body; but there is this most startling fact that he who has put on the faith of the Cross despises even what is naturally fearful, and for Christ's sake is not afraid of death.'

In our own time, C S Lewis gave an astonishingly bold and famous answer to a question back in the days when we felt the nuclear threat even more urgently than we do now. He was asked what he would do if he knew that an atom bomb had been launched. He replied that in the brief time before the dropping and detonation of the bomb, it would be possible to say, 'Poo! You're only a bomb. I'm an immortal soul!' It takes some doing to be able truthfully to say that.

In his book *Christians and the New Africa,* T A Beetham introduced us to Yona, a pastor in Rwanda when inter-tribal fighting broke out in 1963. He knew he was a marked man but he refused to leave his post for a more remote village. One evening he was taken from his home by soldiers and shot at a bridge where the invaders had fought with the national army. Two others taken with him by the soldiers were set free, his bearing in face of death having apparently shamed their captors. They were all amazed; they had never seen anyone go singing to his death, or walking, as he did, like a man just taking a stroll. In being taken out of the army jeep at the bridge, he had asked permission to write in his diary. He wrote: 'We are going to heaven'; and then added, as completely as he could in the time, an account of the church's funds left in his house.

12
Mend, repair, restore

Landlubber as I am, I don't know whether or not fisherfolk find the mending of nets a chore and a bore. I have no doubt that it had to be regularly done to support the Galilean fishing trade. In the days of Jesus the Lake, though set today in a rural landscape, was surrounded by nine cities, each with about 15,000 inhabitants. I learn that men like Zebedee, father of James and John, ran a thriving export business, furnishing the tables of the well-to-do 'in Rome, not least those of the imperial palace, with high-grade fish caught in the Galilean waters. There was a pickling factory at Taricheae (the word means 'pickling places') where the fish were cured.

We read in the Gospels that when Jesus came along the shore to recruit James and John, they were busy with their father in a boat *mending their nets* (Matthew 4: 21). Here, surely, is a detail which adds an authentic touch to the narrative.

Nets need regular repair, we suppose, through sheer wear and tear on sharp rocks and possibly jagged obstructions lying hidden just below the water level. Even an unusually good catch might be weighty enough to damage nets. Luke 5: 6 records just such an incident when the huge capture of fish caused the nets to split; although John preserves a post-Resurrection story of another heavy catch in which 'the net was not torn'.

Having written the foregoing, I yawned. It seemed trivial and a bit dull. But then, like the farmer treading his field without immediately realizing the archaeological treasure buried beneath him, I opened my Greek New Testament and discovered that the word, translated there as 'mending', is a word carrying a variety of meanings. William Barclay labelled it 'the word of Christian discipline'. It means 'to adjust, to put in order, to restore'. That last word is weightier than 'mend' or even 'repair'. Moreover, it moves our attention from nets to us human beings.

Yes, we humans need mending too. The poet Cowper wrote of 'mending mankind'; and Alexander Pope said that it was 'to mend the heart' that 'the Tragic Muse first trod the stage'. I find that the apostle Paul, writing to the churches of Galatia, tells his readers how to exercise Christian discipline. 'If anyone is caught doing wrong,' he states, 'you, my friends, who live by the Spirit must gently put him right.' (Galatians 6: 1) Those last three words in the Greek are translated by the selfsame word for 'mend'.

Mend, repair and restore – here is a ladder of excellence emerging from our rich Greek word. Dads in the home *mend* their children's toys. Professionals in the workshop *repair* faulty machinery. I recall some time ago coming across a notice on the side of a van which read 'We repair what your husband mended!' When we reach the word 'restore', we move up higher in the scale of excellence. Health, paintings and buildings are *restored*. Michel Quoist in his book *With Open Mind* writes of 'Jesus Christ restoring to the world the full weight of Love, of which man robbed it through his sin'. Pope caught the measure of us in his celebrated *Essay on Man* in 1733. We are such a mixture of good and bad, of strength and weakness, a 'Chaos of Thought and Passion . . . Great Lord of all things, yet a prey to all . . . The glory, jest and riddle of the world', yet 'ransomed, healed, *restored*, forgiven'.

Prompted by this picture of those 'Sons of Thunder', Zebedee's boys, mending their nets, I am reminded of a Roman Catholic priest I knew during my Watford days.

One afternoon, I sat in his dining room over a cup of tea and a chocolate biscuit. I was after material for a press profile of him, and he told me about his life. In the fireplace rather threateningly there stood a curved Samurai sword with which he was known to chase thieves from his church if ever they came to rifle the money boxes.

Father John Bebb had graduated in commerce from the London School of Economics. He was all set for a business career as a foreign exchange dealer. Then came the war in 1939. It altered the course of his life, drastically. Commissioned in the Suffolk Regiment, he was quite a lad, known by his colonel as 'that unscrupulous Papist'. On Friday the 13th in 1942, he found himself precariously poised on the brink of death in a far-eastern village.

Lying flat at the mercy of nine Japanese tanks, the young lieutenant, hitherto carefree, experienced what he described as 'ten minutes of the utmost truthfulness' before he was taken prisoner for the next three and a half years. 'I was given a divine kick in the pants in the right direction,' he told me. 'I reviewed my life. It was like looking down on the world from an aeroplane. I felt I was being given a second chance to make something of my life.' From then on, he explained, everything seemed to work out. 'My fiancee at home,' he went on, 'gave me up for dead and married someone else. I was free for the priesthood, and I never thought for a moment I wouldn't survive.'

John Bebb, who doubled his Hertfordshire congregation and later became a talented, award-winning religious broadcaster on TV, needed to be 'mended, repaired, restored' and prepared for a life in the Lord's service. And that's the point. The whole purpose of net maintenance in the fishing business is to enable the nets to be taken out into the deep again and again, day by day, in the pursuit of catch after catch.

Sailing through his years as a divinely commissioned catcher of people, the late John Bebb may well have experienced further 'minutes of the utmost truthfulness' at the hands of his Maker. In the economy of heaven, our dealings with the Lord who kicks us in the right direction need to be renewed again and again. Christian discipleship isn't a 'one-off' enterprise for any of us. We renew and rededicate, start afresh. Sinners as we are, we soon lose the power and enthusiasm of our original commitment and stand constantly in need of new beginnings, top-ups of the Spirit to fuel the service we give to church and world.

Not that I am recommending 'petrol-station Christianity'. Let me explain.

When he was BBC Religious Affairs Correspondent Gerald Priestland used to say that, while caring has been nationalized, faith has become privatized. He claimed that people when cornered would say, 'What I believe is my own business.' But this often conceals a spiritual laziness: no need to bother with church, attend public worship, give money or other help to the missionary task. Thereby the church goes broke, and though founded upon a rock, the ship of faith founders upon the rocks.

There are those who attend public worship yet still keep their faith private, and as a self-centred Sunday fillip or fill-up. 'Padre,' they explain at the church door, 'I come to church once a week to recharge my spiritual batteries.' But Archbishop George Carey, in his younger days, would reply: 'There is no future in petrol-station Christianity – using Sunday to fill the spiritual tank for the week.'

I am a victim of Parkinson's disease and have been since the mid-1980s. I am completely dependent on taking a daily dozen of drugs to keep me on the move. Like scores of other folk who suffer from a whole lot of health problems as they grow older, I need to phone the surgery for repeat prescriptions as my medication runs out.

Is there not a repeat prescription for spiritual health, a regular return to the Lord as we seek the renewal of our inner strength, deriving from faith, hope and love as we continue to serve?

While considering these important matters, I happened to be looking through my copy of the Church Hymnary, the Presbyterian book first published in 1898 and 1927, its third edition appearing in 1973. Hymn 387, I discovered, is a metrical version of the Twenty-Third Psalm. The first line of the second verse reads: 'My soul he doth restore again.' Again? There doesn't seem to be an 'again' in this context in the Bible. The AV has 'He restoreth my soul.' But, as C S Lewis pointed out in his starkly clear-cut way: 'Relying on God has to begin all over again, every day, as if nothing had yet been done.'

13
What kind of cargo?

The long-running TV series University Challenge transmitted a one-off reunion edition some years ago. The idea was to test the expertise of the supposed intelligentsia. They invited back four celebrities who had taken part in the game when they were students. Under the chairmanship of an older, greying and rather less self-assured Bamber Gascoigne, the four had to pit their wits against a team of present-day undergraduates.

Among the celebrities was the tall, ex-Cambridge actor and writer Stephen Fry. As it turned out, he was the one who knew all the answers and so swept his team to a decisive victory. One question was from the Bible. What did King Solomon's fleet bring back in addition to gold, silver and ivory? Instantly Fry's buzzer went and he said, 'Apes and peacocks.' The newer translations have 'monkeys' or 'baboons' for 'peacocks'. No matter. Stephen Fry, a little surprisingly perhaps, knew the answer. How many church members would know it offhand?

King Solomon had, among just about everything else, a considerable mercantile marine. Unusual, this, for the Jews were dedicated landlubbers. They hated the sea. How significant is that description in the Book of Revelation about the new heaven and the new earth. No more sea, said the writer. Perhaps it was just that he was fed up with the sight of nothing but ocean as he looked out across the waters from his cave of exile on the island of Patmos. Still, his heavenly ideal for this world, as much as for the next, was all land. solid and reasonably safe terra firma. The ocean, with its mysterious and somewhat sinister depths, was best avoided. Yet it wasn't just the perils of an unruly and destructive sea which nowadays causes oil to pour into its troubled waters and created a tsunami to kill thousands. In mid-eastern mythology, the sea was thought to be the home of a Loch Ness Monster, the generator of primaeval chaos, the enemy of God.

Sea-fearing rather than sea-faring they may have been in those faraway days. They usually left the maritime life to the Phoenicians who have been described as the 'celebrated navigators' of the ancient Mediterranean world. Nevertheless they themselves sailed the high seas for Solomon. The fleet went out on three-year voyages, venturing perhaps as far as Spain to the west (that's Tarshish, the equivalent of our Timbuctoo in the old saying), and the upper eastern reaches of Africa to the south (Somalia today).

Imagine the anticipatory excitement at the end of the three years. Slowly over the skyline the ships poke their prows. Questions buzz along the wharves. Where have they been this time? How have they fared? Has everyone come back? And, of course, what kind of cargo in the holds? The answer: gold, silver, ivory, apes and monkeys. Solomon expects his merchant sailors to risk their lives for these, a cargo designed merely to make a king, already rich in worldly things, to be richer still, and to entertain him.

There is a fascination about cargoes. John Masefield shared it and wrote a poem plainly entitled 'Cargoes'. He imagined the Quinquireme 'rowing home to haven in sunny Palestine' with its cargo of exotic creatures and 'sandalwood, cedarwood, and sweet white wine'. He also raved over the dirty British coaster with a very different industrial cargo of Tyne coal and 'firewood, iron-ware and cheap tin trays'.

Cargoes can teach us a lesson or two. One has to do with *the wise use of space.*

A ship's hold can take only a limited and carefully balanced cargo. It is so easy to load up with luxuries and forget the necessities, to cram life full of gold and apes leaving no room for the bread of life and living water. Bread and water, physical necessities; but terms to signify also the essentials of the spiritual life. 'I am the bread of life,' said Jesus. To that Samaritan woman beside the well he said: 'Whoever drinks the water that I will give him will become in him a spring which will provide him with life-giving water and give him eternal life' (John 4: 13).

On our life voyage, we need to be sure to load up the hold with what we need and not just with what we want. They will tell you 'down under' that a major disaster of Australian history was a tragedy of overloading. Around 1860 Robert

O'Hara Burke was appointed to lead an expedition into the interior. With him went W J Wills as surveyor and astronomical observer plus fifteen horses, sixteen camels and an immense load. It came to grief months later at Cooper's Creek. They died in the desert overladen.

It alarms me to think that my days and years may be overladen with the wrong things leaving me no space for the cultivation of mind and spirit. 'Blessed are they who are glad to have time to spare for God.'

Lesson two to learn from King Solomon's cargoes has to do with *values*.

Our cargoes, what we carry with us through life and look upon as priorities, judge us. What lay below decks on the merchant ships of Israel over a thousand years BC indicates the prevailing values in high circles in those days of overflowing luxury for the privileged and slave labour for the rest. Look at the goods cluttering up those vessels when the poor in the kingdom could have done with supplies of aid.

Amid the ruins of Pompeii you may look at the macabre figures of its citizens preserved for all these centuries under a blanket of protective volcanic ash. Among them is the woman whose hands clutched pearls, diamonds, rubies, sapphires, gold brooches and earrings worth a number of fortunes laid out in a line today. They say that she held back when the dread warning was given in AD79. She had to gather her riches at all costs. She might have reached safety but she was too late. The rich lady of Pompeii died, as probably she had lived, clinging greedily to her jewels. Didn't she know that in an emergency, when making an exit from a dangerous place at top speed, an orange could be considerably more valuable than all her 'rocks', as the Americans call them?

There is an ancient Persian legend about a man travelling through the desert. He was with others in caravan, but he strayed from it and found himself stranded and alone. He plodded on, lost under a hot sun. He grew thirsty and longed for water. When he had grown desperate, his very life endangered, he spotted what appeared to be a water-skin. With a tremendous effort he dragged himself toward it. He tore it open. No water, not a drop to drink. It was a bag of pearls, completely useless just then.

One of the criminals who took part in the Great Train Robbery was Ronald 'Buster' Edwards. Phil Collins portrayed him, a small-time thief on the run, in a film about the crime entitled *Buster*. His share of the haul enabled him and his family to go and live in luxury on a permanent beach holiday in Acapulco. A hellish prospect I would have thought. That's what Buster's wife, played by Julie Walters soon felt. Things came to a head at Christmas, celebrated (if such is the right word) in Mexican heat. She and their daughter defected. They flew home to the East End with its welcoming grey skies, rain and fog. Buster followed, gave himself up, completed his prison sentence and became an honest-to-goodness flower seller on the Embankment till his death some years ago.

Buster Edwards and his family learned the lesson of right values the hard if not the hardest way. Life consists, as Jesus claimed, not in riches but in relationships, not in luxury but in love, not in gold, silver or even in apeing the jet set, in monkeying about or in lazing on golden beaches and wasting life away.

14

Where they take you in

Was Jesus homeless? Could he be categorized as of no fixed abode? It looks like it, once he had set out on his mission. He and his men walked from Galilee to Jerusalem, a journey of several days. When he sent an advanced party to book bed and breakfast in a Samaritan village, it was no go. No host would give them hospitality because they were heading for hated Jerusalem. Jews and Samaritans were just then at loggerheads. We suppose that the party must have slept rough, under the stars, at least at that stage of their journey. When someone approached Jesus and pledged him total support, he was warned of the likely hardships. 'Foxes have holes, and birds have nests,' Jesus said to him, 'but the Son of Man has nowhere to lie down and rest.' Yes, Jesus was homeless. (Luke 9: 58)

There's no place like home. 'Home,' wrote Robert Frost, 'is the place where, when you have to go there, they take you in.' To this, another replies: 'I should have called it something you somehow haven't to deserve.'

Shades here of the Prodigal Son. That priceless story illustrates experiences to do with home that, sometime or another, early or late, young or old, fall upon us all. For example, we all know what it is to *leave* home.

Only a few TV commercials, out of the thousands broadcast each year, do we remember for long afterwards. I recall one from years ago set in an airport lounge. Husband and father is off to the far side of Canada as part of his job. Wife doesn't want him to go. There is a tearful farewell. The product being advertised was Kleenex tissues! The scene is commonplace, whether it's at an airport, on a station platform or at the front door of the old homestead. We all leave home at some time.

The small boy or girl off to boarding school for the first time; the sailor, soldier, airman off on a tour of duty, maybe abroad, maybe to face danger. Or, the young woman or man leaving home for good to be married and to create a new home. These are milestone experiences along our earthly pathway as we walk down the garden path perhaps for ever.

One of the most poignant home-leaving scenes in recent times was movingly presented on television. It was the dark but inevitable day when Hannah Hauxwell had to move out of her life's home, the austere and remote Yorkshire farmhouse where she'd lived alone without electricity or water and withstood sixty bleak and severe winters in increasing poverty and squalor. She couldn't be allowed to continue. She'd die in her tracks as she dragged hay across the snow to feed her beloved beasts. Her friends arranged a comfortable cottage for her in the village of Cotherstone. We saw her leaving the farm for ever, sitting in the tractor which hauled the furniture van through the snow. Her dog Timmy was with her, but her face wet with tears said it all. 'Wherever I am, whatever I am,' she said, 'a big part of me will be left here. Nowhere else...'

Whatever the circumstances, leaving home is an experience to be set alongside birth and death.

To continue: we all know what it is to *miss* home. Nostalgia is a much misused word. It doesn't mean wistfully hankering after the past but painfully longing for home. Haven't we all suffered homesickness?

Nearly a thousand years BC, an Old Testament character named Hadad in the days of King Solomon fled to Egypt for protection, a refugee in the royal court. He says to the Pharaoh: 'Let me go back to my own country.' Why? Had his host failed to give him something?   Was that why he had wanted to go back home? No, it wasn't that. Hadad simply replied, 'Just let me go.' He was the ruler of Edom south of the Dead Sea. He was homesick. (1 Kings 11: 21)

In his harrowing novel *One day in the life of Ivan Denisovich*, Alexander Solzhenitsyn introduces his readers to Shukov, a prisoner in the Gulag, gazing at the ceiling of his cell in silence and discussing freedom with Aloysha. 'Now he didn't know... whether he wanted freedom or not,' it says. 'At first he'd longed for it. Every night he'd counted the days of his stretch ... and then he'd grown bored with counting. Then it became clear that men of his like wouldn't ever be allowed to return home, that they'd be exiled ... Freedom meant one thing to him – home. *But they wouldn't let him go home.* ' A terrible plight!

Anyone would want to go anywhere away from a Siberian prison. But to be homesick means to find even the most beautiful and civilized place barren and empty. Think of Robert Browning in Italy watching the buds come in. But he cries, 'Oh, to be in England now that April's there.' Think of Rupert Brooke in Berlin with his cry of homesickness: 'Would I were in Grantchester, in Grantchester!'

Strange would we be if we couldn't understand these cries, if we had never had the experience of missing home. And we surely know what it is to *return* home.

The song-writers on a large scale have tuned into the basic emotions felt by us all at the prospect of returning home and of actually doing so. Remember that First World War song 'Keep the home fires burning'? When American troops were expected home from Vietnam, 'Tie a Yellow Ribbon round the Old Oak Tree' topped the 1973 pop charts on both sides of the Atlantic. Long before Tom Jones popularized 'Green, Green Grass of Home' it was a Country and Western classic. We all readily identify with its sentiments as the man (has he been in prison?) steps off the train, views the familiar sights and people, and feels beneath his feet the green, green grass of home.

Haven't we all known the joy of returning home? How many Britishers have found the sight of the white cliffs of Dover, like a sight of heaven?

Let's look at Jesus. He *left* home to prosecute his mission. We may guess that he *missed* home, for he was yet a man with human feelings. We believe that in a profoundly mysterious way, when he died, was raised and ascended to heaven, he *returned* home.

If you've seen the Oberammergau Passion Play, you will have noticed that much is made of the departure of Jesus from home, or, at any rate, from his mother Mary. There is a dialogue between Jesus and Mary. 'Mother, Mother!' he says. 'Receive the thanks of your Son for your love and maternal care which you have shown me in the thirty-three years of my life. My Father calls me. Farewell, beloved Mother.'

There is no scriptural basis for any such scene. None of the Gospel writers make any reference to any such thing, although the Fourth Gospel shows Jesus, as he dies in agony on the cross, commending his mother to the care of John. Nevertheless, Jesus seemed to disown his own kith and kin; and he did say that a man's worst enemies would be members of his own family. Did Jesus leave home under a cloud? There is some scriptural basis for assuming so. When word went around that the young carpenter from Nazareth, now an itinerant preacher, had taken leave of his senses, his mother and brothers went out to bring him home, but he seemed to leave them in the lurch.

Finally and eventually, Jesus returned home, though not to Nazareth. In the Upper Room in his farewell speech he told his disciples that he was going to the Father whence he had come, and he was going to prepare a place for them in his Father's house.

We live for a limited time in this world, but we belong to another kingdom which is why we sometimes feel alone in a crowd and lost with a sort of homesickness afflicting us. Long ago, the Psalmist said, 'Lord, you have always been our home', which is why St Augustine left us that classic prayer: 'Thou hast made us for thyself, O God, and our hearts are restless until they find their rest in thee.'

15

What kind of fool am I?

You won't find any collect for All Fools' Day in the Book of Common Prayer. It isn't a Christian festival but a pre-Christian custom. We don't know how the practice of playing tricks on people began. We do know that India from time immemorial has had its spring festival of Huli noted for its tricks and pranks. France had such a custom as far back as the sixteenth century. The victim of the practical joking was known as an 'April fish' – *Poisson d'Avril.* And we have our April fools.

The Bible is full of fools; or, rather, of the word 'fool'. Let's go looking for some of them.

In Psalm 14, 'Fools say in their hearts, "There is no God".' Here is *the folly of blatant unbelief.*

These fools, according to Hebrew scholars, aren't the stupid, unthinking ones, but those who are morally perverse and arrogant. One commentary uses the words 'deliberate' and 'blatant'. There are highly intelligent and cultured men and women who deny God.

I have read somewhere a double definition of atheism. It isn't only a doubt that God exists: it may also be *a will to have no God,* Mind you, there are those who feel, sometimes intensely, the pain of their unbelief and who envy the believers?

Belonging to this category is the broadcaster John Humphrys. In an interview in *Night & Day,* the weekly magazine of *The Mail on Sunday,* he explains that he was brought up to be religious in the Anglican Church in Wales (not Chapel), but any Christian faith he may have had has worn away over time. 'It simply didn't give me the answers,' he stated. He confessed that he was unable to believe in organized religion, in heaven and hell, in a personal God, and that he couldn't imagine any sort of afterlife. Yet he pauses before the phenomenon of conscience in humankind. It puzzles him. It must have developed for a reason, he says.

We who confess Christ and find the way to God through him have a pastoral responsibility to deal carefully with those who suffer the pain of unbelief. In many of our congregations there will be the believing wives of unbelieving husbands, and it's usually that way round. I remember a middle-aged couple where she was a busy leading churchwoman while he, a sensitive sole, struggled with his doubts and felt shut out of her church. With some bitterness he said to me that the Church had stolen her from him. Her brash vicar, on being introduced to him, said brusquely, 'You're an unbeliever, I understand.' Permanent barriers are built from such rough handling.

There are gentler ways of pastoral approach to envious doubters. John Humphrys, who is no fool, blurting out 'There is no God', says that doubt is a heavy burden. 'The hardest way to live is with uncertainty,' he concludes, 'and it must be comforting to have found a meaning to life.'

In Luke 12 at verse 20, we come across the statement: 'But God said to him, "You fool!"' Here is *the folly of complacent materialism*.

The divine voice breaks in as the wealthy businessman, in agriculture by the look of it, tells why he is so pleased with himself. He has managed to expand his business to such an extent that he can afford to retire early. He has achieved what he regards as permanent security. But he is suddenly and chillingly confronted with death, and he is made to realize that far from having everything he has nothing. His mind and energy, we take it, have been so engrossed with the things of this world that he has nothing to take with him into the next.

This story of the rich fool is, of course, one of the parables of Jesus. It is graphic stuff. Just as our business tycoon is relaxing into a life of eating, drinking and merriment, along comes God, calls him a fool and warns him what happens to those who store up treasures for themselves but are not rich toward God.

Life consists, among other things, of getting our priorities right. We learn that what we have and what we do in this world are only of relative value. What we are thus far ('Thus far has the Lord helped us,' said Samuel), and what we become, are of absolute value. Shakespeare put it in his own way. 'If thou art rich, thou art poor; for like an ass whose back with ingots bows, thou bearest thy heavy riches but a journey and death unloads thee.'

Let's be sure to keep the material things in a right perspective. I make a plea to preachers, as one of them myself. Pulpits are wonderful launch pads for ranting about the sins of materialism, complacent or otherwise. The 'things' of this life should be seen as the gift of a generous God rather than as the instruments of the Devil. Through them love is expressed and joy engendered,

A fellow-minister, with whom I shared my college years in Bradford, always sends us Christmas greetings. Brian Baker and his wife Sheila live in retirement in the pleasant county of Rutland, and the first paragraph of their 2004 Christmas round robin expressed it elegantly:

'Down at the supermarket this morning we encountered a transformation. Everything about it announced the coming of Christmas: advent colours, the word "gifts", the glamour of the merchandise – bikes for children, tools for dads, clothes for mums, yummy foods for everyone; uncles, aunts, grandparents – everyone. Oliver Cromwell's followers might have taken an axe to it but, on a dank, cold morning, *we found this materialism cheering.* It told us that this was a season of joy.'

So, unto this last. In First Corinthians 4, missionary Paul is dealing with factional rows within the fellowship at Corinth and he writes: 'We are fools for the sake of Christ.' Here we find *the folly of Christian commitment.*

When ex-slave ship captain John Newton wrote his hymn 'Glorious things of thee are spoken' in the 1770s, he must have been well aware how the world, looking on at the church community, tended to deride and pity the Christians as fools. The twentieth century looked on at two extra-special Christians who demonstrated what Christian commitment really means. Albert Schweitzer and Mother Teresa were fools for Christ's sake, writ large.

Born in 1875 in Alsace, Schweitzer was an outstanding theologian, philosopher and musician with three doctorates to his name, and destined to be a Nobel Prize Winner. He learned to play the organ under Charles Widor who composed that Toccata and Fugue which is the Mount Everest of organ playing. Schweitzer became a concert artiste and musicologist, writing an authoritative study of J S Bach. He also penned an essay on organ building. He served as a curate at St Nicholas Church, Strasbourg and, from 1903, as principal of the theological college. His plan was to devote his energies to science and art till he was thirty, and then to give himself wholeheartedly to the service of humanity. Suddenly, however, he announced that he was going to study medicine, qualify as a surgeon, and go to Central Africa to fight dysentery, leprosy and sleeping sickness. He might have gone to India, Samoa or Greenland, but he picked up a mission magazine in which he read an article which changed his mind. Qualifying in 1913, he took his wife with him to set up a hospital at Lambarene a deserted mission station in French Equatorial Africa. Inevitably he was criticized for turning his back on the brilliant career he could have had in Europe. He was, in the eyes of the world, a fool.

So was Mother Teresa. She was born in Yugoslavia of Albanian parents in 1910. Travelling to India in 1928, she taught at a convent school in Calcutta and joined the Irish Order of Sisters of Lorreto. She became principal of the school, but in 1948 she left the school to work alone in the slums of the city. She took a week-long course in basic nursing; and, joined by other nuns, she opened her House for the Dying in 1952. She was awarded the Nobel Peace Prize in 1971. 'The biggest disease today,' she said, 'is not leprosy or tuberculosis, but rather the feeling of being unwanted.' Mother Teresa was unworldly but down to earth. She once asked an airline, to fly her to Europe free, to save the fare for her work in Calcutta in exchange for her services as an airline steward. They declined the offer. Like Schweitzer she renounced earthly comforts, turned her back on a far easier life, and all to help people who couldn't be saved and would die soon afterwards. But, like Schweitzer, it was for Christ's sake that she was a fool.

Years ago, there was a musical show in London entitled *Stop the World – I Want To Get Off*. The show-stopping song was 'What kind of fool am I? '

We may well ask ourselves that question.

16
Being there

The last and perhaps the least successful film which Peter Sellers made was *Being There* in 1980. He played a feeble-minded gardener whose entire knowledge of life came from watching television. I came by the video as a free gift from Dixon's for buying one of their video cassette recorders. As you might expect, the movie was hardly worth having for keeps. It would have been astonishing to say the least if they had been giving away *The Sound of Music*

Some years earlier, T S Eliot had defined TV as 'a medium of entertainment which permits millions of people to listen to the same joke at the same time, and yet remain lonesome'.

Never mind this wisdom nor the film, but look at the title. It drives me to my Bible. In Psalm 139 the Psalmist says of God: 'If I flew away beyond the east or lived in the farthest place in the west, *you would be there* to lead me ... to help me.'

I've been rolling that film title around in my mind. 'Being There' may not have been much of a movie but its title provokes many a useful thought. I hasten to share a few of them with you.

We can say that by Being There, God provides us with *the strength of inner resources*.

We like to think that God is there for that. Nonetheless, the notion of his all-pervading presence has an unwelcome side to it. 'The Lord sees what happens everywhere,' it states in Proverbs; 'he is watching us, whether we do good or evil.' This, the Big Brother aspect of God, is an unpopular view of Deity, yet it's there in holy scripture.   Linaeus, the Swedish botanist, had a Latin inscription over the door of his lecture room which said: 'Live innocently; God is here.'

That Psalm 139 isn't only a song of comfort in the omnipresence of God. It is an articulation of awe, even of some alarm, at the thought of his omniscience too.   Lord, you know me, you know everything I do, you understand all my thoughts, you know all my actions. Where could I go to escape from you, to get away from your presence? Escape? I am like a prisoner broken free who does a 'runner', but is soon recaptured. There's no getting away from God at all.

This Psalm before us was traditionally set in the Church's Burial Service for those who committed suicide. A minister tells how a girl in deep distress telephoned him, and without giving her name, said: 'I am going to commit suicide. Only one thing is holding me back, and I want you to give me an honest answer. Will I have to face God after I am dead?' The minister told her to read Psalm 139. God isn't waiting far away on the other side of the Ultimate. He is here and now.

Still, the reassuring truth remains. God provides us with inner resources for us to tap when we're in trouble. Charles Wesley bade the soldiers of Christ arise and put their armour on, 'strong in the strength which God supplies through his eternal Son'.

We can also say that by Being There the Church demonstrates *the power of silent witness.*

As the Soviet state came to its welcome end under the brave leadership of Mikhail Gorbachev, crowds thronged Red Square in the name of democratic freedom. We watched it open-mouthed on our TV screens never expecting to see such a thing actually come to pass. And my heart leapt when I saw, as you surely did, the sight of a crucifix rising up from the midst of that huge throng. It was a moving sight. *The Church was there.*

Those old tyrants and oppressors, the hard men of the Kremlin, had done their damnedst over the years to suppress the Church and wipe out the religious vision with their pathetic Anti-God Movement. But all the time, all the way through, the Church was there; and here it was, with the supreme symbol of Christian faith rising up in resurrection triumph above the heads of that crowd, almost mocking the folly of those who thought they could put it down for good.

It's the same story in Communist China. Colin Thubron in his book *Behind the Wall*, a graphic account of a journey he made across that vast country, relates how he attended a Sunday morning service at the Protestant church at Nanjing. It was the mid-eighties, and that church had only been reopened three weeks earlier as a result of the ending of the Cultural Revolution.

It was packed out with a congregation of four hundred, many of them clerks, students and factory workers, Mr Thubron's neighbour whispered to him in English: 'The sermon concerns Eternal Life.' Afterwards this man, a middle-aged missionary priest, asked the author back to his office for a glass of boiling tea.

There Colin Thubron heard how so many church buildings had been taken over by the Maoist regime and used as schools, factories and even living quarters. Now they were gradually being retrieved, a lengthy and difficult process. This priest explained that 3,500 churches had reopened, and some ten thousand assembly points for worship had been established.

Suppressed and driven underground, the Church had nevertheless been there. Jesus had so promised. His Church is built upon a rock, and the powers of death shall never conquer it.

By Being There, we may all exercise *the ministry of a supporting presence.*

Remember Robert Dougall, BBC tv newsreader thirty years ago? In his autobiography *In and Out of the Box* he referred to some of the letters he used to get. Like the one from the lady who asked him if he liked the colour of the new curtains in her sitting room. Are there still people who really do believe that the newsreader can see them? Or, Mr Dougall suggested, is this a symptom of something more fundamental? Is it that in the midst of so much change and upheaval, the newsreader embodies continuity and stability?

The family doctor and the vicar once provided this kind of security. Even the small shopkeeper helped, his shop always being reliably there at the corner of the road, like the parish church, the surgery and the village inn. Lonely people, wrote Robert Dougall, look to an electronic image for reassurance. He is almost incredulous, he declared, when someone writes to say how much he has helped them at a difficult time. 'How can you help a person by just giving out the news on television?' he asked. 'But this has happened so many times that I can only think it is because they can at least rely on my *being there.*'

When some crisis looms up, some trouble hits us, there are dedicated, responsible people who enter the situation to provide some service: the doctor, the policeman, the solicitor, the undertaker. Each has his specific job to do. But there are others who don't actually do anything. They are just *there.* And you need them there. You want them to be around, to stand beside you, to give you moral support. Ministers often fulfil this function. Sometimes we are at a loss to know what we can do, what we can say, in a given situation. Whereas we have a vital work to do in just being there.

Remember Leslie Cooke, a commanding ecumenical leader and outstanding preacher? I can see him now, in that bandstand of a pulpit, preaching in Westminster Chapel in London. 'Over large parts of the world,' he said at the time, 'it is no longer for the Church to engage in mission as we have understood it; you may not make a convert. Over large parts of the world it is not possible for the Church to engage in works of mercy, in caring for the aged, the sick, the widowed and the orphaned.' Then he added: 'These very restrictions force us back upon the essential task of the Church which is to *be there, a* Christian presence, carrying by its intercessions and its sacramental life the sins and sorrows of the world, and carrying them redemptively and reconcilingly.'

17

A knock at the door

'Not many sounds in life, and I include all urban and rural sounds,' wrote Charles Lamb, 'exceed in interest a knock at the door.' Who would disagree with that observation? Think of all the reasons for the knock, or, today, for the sound of the doorbell. Think of the differing emotions aroused in those within by such a sound, whether it's a ting-a-ling or a rattatat. The classic example may be found after Macbeth has murdered Duncan and, amid unbearable tension, he cries out: 'Whence is that knocking? How is't with me, when every noise appals me?' So, when the author of the puzzling Book of Revelation shows us the Lord himself knocking at a door, we appreciate the powerful appeal of the image.

A knock at the door may bring good cheer and uplift when we're low and in despair. It may be the postman with a parcel of surprises enough to lift the dark clouds for you. It may be an unexpected visitor who changes your view of things and is a heavenly blessing. It may be the police with bad or even grave news. And some callers can be a nuisance if not a menace.

In 1854 when he was in his late twenties, the Pre-Raphaelite artist Holman Hunt painted his famous allegorical representation of Christ knocking at the door of the human soul. Its title is 'The Light of the World.' There stands the figure of Jesus Christ, a cloak over his shoulders, a crown of thorns on his head, and a brightly shining lantern in his left hand. With his right hand he knocks at a door. Quoted under the picture is the text from Revelation chapter three that we associate with this painting... 'Behold, I stand at the door, and knock ... '

We like to imagine the risen Lord approaching each of us gently, knocking at our door, appealing to us to follow him, seeking to persuade us to consider joining the company of his disciples. He does not coerce or compel us to fall in behind him. The artist, they say, wished to make it clear that there is no handle on the door. Holman Hunt was thereby emphasizing that the means of admittance is on the inside. The Lord cannot come in unless we inside lift the handle for him to enter. His entry is in our control.

One hymn among many in *Congregational Praise* which haven't been carried over into *Rejoice and Sing* (I have no complaints!) is Joseph Grigg's 'Behold a stranger at the door!' It first appeared in all its eleven verses ten or twelve years after Hunt's painting first saw daylight. The first verse tells of the stranger gently knocking, and waiting a long time for the door to be opened. The last line of that opening verse says, 'You treat no other friend so ill.' He stands there in a lovely attitude with melting heart and matchless kindness, to quote Grigg's phrases. Yet even in this hymn written by an eighteenth-century Essex man, towards the end a sterner tone is introduced. At verse four, we are reminded that when Christ comes he comes to reign, thoughts that disobey must be slain. He is the King of kings who, although his is a gentle reign, a reign it is nonetheless.

Interestingly, the Greek word for 'knock' here doesn't indicate a gentle tap. It means to strike, to smite, to thump. It means a knocking not so much with the knuckles as with a staff, somewhat like a bishop pounding ceremonially at the cathedral door with his staff when he comes to be installed in his *cathedra*. Jesus Christ comes to us, never to break down the door of our hearts but to wake us up to a decision to admit him or not. Sydney Carter wrote a Christmas song, 'Knocking on the window'. It ended like this:

> *Till you woke us with your knocking,*
> *We were sleeping like the dead, sir.*

A quick glance at Holman Hunt's painting isn't enough. Nor is it wise to reject the work as a piece of outmoded Victoriana to be sniffily dismissed. There are subtleties in it that require careful observation.

One day about eighty years ago, a couple were standing before this painting in St Paul's Cathedral and talking quietly about it. Lurking nearby like Professor Higgins behind a pillar of the church in the old Covent Garden in the opening scone of *My Fair Lady*, a stranger approached them. He apologized for having overheard what they had been saying. 'I knew Holman Hunt pretty well,' he told them; 'indeed, I was with him a good deal in the days when he was engaged upon the work before you. And really, if you will pardon my saying so, you have completely missed one of the main ideas that he had in mind.' At their request, the stranger went on to enlarge upon the subject.

The artist had painted a tangle of undergrowth on the ground and around the door to indicate that the house was standing on the fringe of the wilderness. The Saviour is about to leave the open country, bathed in moonlight, and to plunge into the shadowed gloom of that dark region. It is for this purpose that he has lit and is carrying the lantern. He is knocking at the door, not merely in the hope of being admitted and having supper with those within, but also *and mainly to* invite them to join him on his missionary journey through the world's darkness.

You and I are naturally attracted to the Jesus who says, 'Come to me, all who are weary and whose load is heavy; I will give you rest.' We are less comfortable when we hear him say, 'Go therefore to all nations and make them my disciples.' The invitation to rest is considerably more desirable than the call to mission and service. Both the 'come' and the 'go' are essential ingredients of the gospel. People should be able to find a comforting of their troubled hearts in every church. But there is also the demand upon us to 'go'. God can be tough, hard upon his supporters and workers.

Poor old Elijah! His life threatened by the wicked Jezebel, he runs away. He goes a day's journey into the wilderness. He is full of self-pity, is even suicidal. Dead tired, he sleeps, only to find food and drink supplied to him upon waking. 'Rise and eat,' an angel directs him; 'the journey is too much for you.' This is the 'come to me' bit. Spending the night in a cave, however, Elijah is less comfortingly handled by the Lord who asks him 'Why are you here, Elijah?' And the next word is 'go'. 'Go back by way of the wilderness of Damascus, enter the city, and anoint Hazael to be king ... and Elisha ... to be prophet in your place' (I Kings 19), It is as if God is saying to him, 'Don't expect to be mollycoddled in your self-pity. You've work to do for me.'

Two of the four sons that Mary Craig brought to birth were handicapped, the first exceedingly so. In her book *Blessings* she writes of reaching the point of exhaustion and angry with God for leaving her to cope. She felt she had to get away. As a Catholic she went to the Sue Ryder Home in the Suffolk village of Cavendish. 'I had come to indulge in a bout of do-gooding,' she confessed, 'and was all dressed up to play the role of lady bountiful.' She had offered her services bed-making, cooking, whatever.

No sooner had Mary set foot in 'the idyllic, pink-washed sixteenth-century house' than she was confronted with the cry, 'Thank God you've come ... you must be the new slave.' Immediately she was plunged into a crisis. Then a flooded bathroom had to be cleared up, supper for seventy prepared; and jobs like peeling hundredweights of potatoes and heating gallons of soup.

Mary Craig described Sue Ryder as 'a tiny bird-like woman who looks vulnerable but is about as fragile as granite'. Travelling to Poland with her in a large Austin van, Mary told of cramped discomfort, snatched sleep and little to eat. Baroness Ryder was totally unsympathetic with her complaints and tersely replied, 'You ought to be with me in winter.'

It was in Cavendish that Mary Craig, Oxford graduate in French, learned her major life-changing lesson: how to deal with one's personal suffering. USE IT. 'Use it,' she stated, 'for the hungry, the homeless, the lonely; for the man down the road who's lost both his job and his wife; for the friend whose little girl has been killed. Use it to help me understand, to be less self-centred, more loving.' It is in sorrow, she claimed, that we discover ourselves and what really matters. She quotes Ernest Hemingway who is said to have written to Scott Fitzgerald: 'When you get the damned hurt, use it. Use it and don't cheat.'

It is to show us this way that the Lord knocks at our door.

18

Take this baby

A religious quiz question might be this: when was a mother a nanny to her own child? It isn't a catch question. The answer lies in the first nine verses of Exodus chapter two.

Over three millennia ago in Egypt, the Pharaoh ordered the extermination of newly-born Hebrew males, much as Herod hundreds of years later demanded the massacre of the under-two boy babies of Bethlehem. The Egyptian king was afraid that the little sons of his Hebrew slaves would grow into too many strong men capable of successful revolt and the overthrow of the Pharaohs. His edict said: 'Take every new-born Hebrew boy and throw him into the Nile, but let all the girls live.'

The mother of a bonny boy to be named Moses (meaning either 'to pull out' or 'child of the river') hid him for three months in a basket among the shallows. The Pharaoh's daughter, humanely inclined, found him while taking a dip and was touched by his crying. To save him from her callous father's infant cull, she had him rescued; and by a smart move typically Jewish, the little lad robust in limb and lung was handed over to a wet-nurse who, unbeknown to the princess, was his mother.

Imagine the tabloids headlining the story: Nile Nanny Was Mummy. But that won't do. They don't have live mummies in Egypt!

To the Hebrew woman she didn't suspect as the rescued child's mother, the princess said: 'Take this baby and nurse him for me, and I will pay you.' Later, his mother would send him back (heart-rending surely) to be royally adopted, and in time to lead the Exodus. The momentous outcome of that riverside discovery need not concern us for now. Share with me the 'filleting' of what the princess said. It would make a statement from the Good News Bible suitable for framing and hanging on the nursery wall.

First, the Gift. *Take this baby.*

Every child is a tailor-made gift from God. There is divine significance in the biological fact, so forensically useful, that each of us has unique finger-prints and, even more amazingly, a distinctive DNA. Our precious individuality in the sight of heaven, thus incorporated into our bodily make-up, casts doubt and commends caution on such issues as abortion and the scientists' itch to experiment with genetic engineering, cloning and the like.

During wartime, Brigadier General Theodore Roosevelt Junior was waiting for a plane when a sailor asked for a seat on the same flight. 'I want to see my mother,' he explained. 'I haven't much time.' The girl at the ticket window shrugged and said, 'There's a war on, you know.'

Overhearing this exchange, the General stepped up and told her to give the sailor his seat. A friend butted in 'Teddy, aren't you in a hurry too?'
'It's a matter of rank,' he replied. 'I'm only a general; he's a son.'

A right sense of values and priorities here!

A chapter comes to mind in one of Bishop Fulton Sheen's books headed 'Holy Terrors'. Children are occasionally so described. The writer commented that the second word is usually given more weight than the first. The 'terror' element in the untamed child needs to be and can be changed for the better by loving discipline. May we not speculate on the boy Jesus here? Was he a model of instant perfection, or did he, even he, need disciplining? To deny that possibility is to question the validity and genuineness of the Incarnation.

A 'holy terror' may be a terror, temporarily, one hopes; but whoever he is, he is intrinsically holy for sure.

Next, the Task: *Nurse him for me.*

To nurse is to nourish. Both words share the same root. In these unisex days, father as well as mother does the nursing. The nourishing, in the earliest stages at least, was intended in the divine plan, or so it looks, to be done by mother alone. She alone is physically equipped to nourish her child both before and after birth.

I love the observation of Felicity aged seven, written in her own fair hand in Nanette Newman's *Lots of love* in the mid-1970s. It was the age of the factory drinks dispenser, and Felicity informs us: 'When you are a baby your mother feeds you from her bozom but she can only do milk.' And, we must add, she *alone*. Father isn't fitted to feed baby unless from a bottle, and not at all antenatally.

Not having seen it myself, I rely on the report that there is, definitely was anyway, a Reynolds portrait of three women in a Cheshire art gallery. When it first arrived at the Lever in Port Sunlight, it had only two of them visible. Lord Leverhulme, intent on collecting 'the best of British' in pottery, furniture, needlework and paintings, acquired the portrait with the signature of Sir Joshua clearly visible in the bottom corner. It was clear that something was wrong said expert opinion. Reynolds, probably England's greatest portrait painter, wouldn't have released a picture like that with the 'balance' so out of true.

They took it to the cleaners, and it came back now with a third figure revealed. Another had painted on the canvas and blotted out, though not irretrievably, the figure of Mrs Paine. She was the mother of the two girls. The balance of the work was now right and indisputably a Reynolds. Mother, or a mother-figure, as nurse and nourisher supreme, is a must.

Lastly, the Reward: *I will pay you,*

In my copy of *The Penguin Dictionary of Modern Humorous Quotations*, there are, I find, nearly thirty quips about children. All are based on the assumption that all children are unholy terrors. 'I never met a kid I liked,' moaned the poor drunken old actor W C Fields. 'Anybody who hates children or dogs can't be all bad.' Not bad, no; but sad, yes.

The young can be a worry and an irritation. 'Youngsters brighten up the home,' remarked one parent, 'especially when they leave all the lights on!' To soothe our furrowed brow in such circumstances, we turn to Psalm 127 and its third verse where we read: 'Children are a gift from the Lord; they are a real blessing.' There are bound to be times when we find that sentiment hard to swallow. Our young may well be a mixed blessing. But in our best moments we would agree with the Italian proverb which says, 'Little children are little sorrows but great joys.' They are a reward from God.

This is true of even handicapped children, as their parents will more than often testify. Mary Craig and her husband have had an exhausting, harrowing time with a family of four sons of whom two turned out to be sub-normal. Nicky is a case of Down's Syndrome. She wrote of them in *Blessings*, a book which is a moving testimony to redemptive suffering. Near the end she wrote: 'Nicky's mental age does not seem all that important to us. What is important is the joy he has brought us. He is the focal point of our family, the most beloved of every one of us ... "I'm glad there was a Paul and a Nicky," a friend of mine suddenly burst out a few weeks ago. By and large, I think I am glad too.'

On Mothering Sunday I reminded our congregation that this particular Sunday in the church calendar was also known as Laetare Sunday. The Latin word means to be glad, joyful, cheerful. It is also said to be a day for visiting the cathedral, the Mother Church. But above all it is the day for honouring mothers and motherhood. I drew the attention of my hearers to Proverbs 30 verse 11 where it says that there are people who do not show their appreciation for their mothers. Also, I quoted Jacqueline Kennedy Onassis who underlined their vital importance when she said to mothers and, we presume, also to fathers: 'If you bungle raising your children I don't think whatever else you do well matters very much.'

19
Pursuit and Discovery

Joyce Grenfell was a keen observer of human foibles, a highly intelligent and sensitive woman, witty and wise. A Christian Scientist, she was also deeply religious in the best sense. The Cardinal Archbishop of Westminster said that she was the most religious person he had ever met.

Among many quotable quotes she left for us to think about, there is this: 'There is no such thing as the pursuit of happiness, there is only the discovery of joy.'

Let me shade in for emphasis two words in that sentence. Not happiness and joy, but pursuit and discovery. Is life a matter of pursuit or a process of discovery?

No doubt you will have noticed the difference between the two men in the Parables of the Hidden Treasure and the Pearl (Matthew 13: 44-45). The one was *looking for* fine pearls. The other *happens to find* a treasure hidden in a field. One was a *pursuer*, the other a *discoverer*. These two very short stories are bang up to date. There are always dealers after precious stones who will pay high prices for the finest; and I knew a farmer in Suffolk, a member of one of our churches, who one day out with his tractor stumbled upon Roman treasure.

Human beings are pursuers. A policeman who belonged to my Bournemouth congregation and patiently gave Margaret and me much driving practice when we were learning over forty years ago, confessed to me that, as a mobile bobby, he loved the thrill of the chase. Perhaps that's what attracts the fox-hunting fraternity rather than the desire to keep the fox population down, a virtuous but dubious plea.

We pursue *sexual fulfilment.* Some land in gaol for doing so. Most marry and have children and live stable and happy lives till death them do part. We derive much amusement from the Creator's little joke in putting this fierce urge within us. What would the humorists and the comedians do without it? How would the world of the arts and the media fare if there were no such pursuit? Could God's experiment with life on this planet continue?

We are bound to acknowledge that the Creator making us thus has burdened us with both blessing and curse, a heady mix of agony and ecstasy; and it's a major feature of life that the Church has historically been unable to cope with.

We pursue *wealth and status.* Some land in gaol for doing so at all costs, especially when their greed cost others dear. Maybe in these days, as the Bishop of Oxford awhile ago suggested, we should be more concerned about what happens in board-rooms than in bedrooms.

Down the centuries wise men have alerted us to the perils of avariciously chasing money for our own selfish ends. Jesus repeatedly did so, warning us that we cannot serve both God and money. All evil, declared the Apostle Paul, stems from a love of money. 'Nothing that is God's is obtainable by money,' claimed Quintus Tertullian two centuries after Christ. A thousand years later still, Bernard of Clairvaux insisted that 'theirs is an endless road, a hopeless maze, who seek for goods before they seek for God'. Endless, too, are the warnings about the dangers inherent in wealth, yet it is hotly pursued, and we measure our priorities and values by it.

We pursue *excellence in learning.* The pursuit of excellence is a phrase used by those who seek a fair deal for the exceptionally gifted child. In our anxiety to offer equal opportunities to all, we may unheedingly neglect the top-of-the-class children who thereby may be held back in a system of enforced mediocrity. We need them as our future leaders. Erich Fromm defined education as 'helping the child realize his potentialities'.

We pursue *happiness.* For Americans, according to their Constitution, its pursuit is an inalienable right. Joyce Grenfell, half-American herself on her mother's side, regarded happiness as something we cannot pursue. It falls into our laps incidentally as we do other things in self-forgetfulness. When he washed their feet, Jesus taught his inner circle of disciples about service. 'Now that you know this truth,' he concluded, 'how happy you will be if you put it into practice.'

Time to turn our attention to that second word, discovery. The Creator has built into his creation, sunk into it, a whole lot of marvels for making man's lot easier, pleasanter and more comfortable. Having done so, he seems to have set humankind the task of finding this treasure trove. The history of science is the account of man's hunt for and discovery of these treasures one by one, with plenty more to come over the inconceivably long time-span in which the Creator appears to be conducting his colossal enterprise with Planet Earth and Homo Sapiens.

Furthermore, some of the most important discoveries have been *accidental*, stumbled upon while other lines of thought and experiment were being tried. It's like the man who *happened to find* a hidden cache in his field. The parable Jesus told to illustrate what the Kingdom of God is like may well have been based on an actual incident. It's as if Jesus had said: 'Did you read in the *Galilean Gazette* about that man who tripped over a treasure chest while he was out working on his land this week?'

Buried treasure wasn't uncommon out there in those days. There were no safes or bank deposit boxes, so folk buried their assets. Then, with war falling upon them and an invading enemy overrunning them, they might need to flee quickly. They would hope to return in due time when things had died down, and peace and stability were restored. But perhaps they'd never come back, and there lay the treasure, unknown till discovered and then claimed on a basis which was the law.

Scientific records are full of discoveries made accidentally.

Around 1800, when he was only in his twenties, Sir Humphrey Davy, curious about the properties of gases, was playing about with nitrous oxide. He breathed it to see what would happen. He noticed that a whiff of it relieved the pain of an aching tooth. At the time nitrous oxide was a fairground plaything. You were invited to step up and breathe it in. It made you laugh hysterically. At an American sideshow, one man was so affected that he fell down and gashed his leg badly, but he seemed not to suffer pain. A watching dentist bought a bottle of this 'laughing gas' and tried it on his patients. Thus painless dentistry was born, and by accident. A century later, in a darkened room in Bavaria, a physics professor was researching how gases conducted electricity, probing the principle now long since used in neon and fluorescent lighting. Out of these experiments and by sheer chance, Conrad Roentgen discovered what we now know as the X-ray. That's what it was called and is still, because Roentgen didn't know how it worked. He simply found that it did.

One could go on. The stories of accidental discovery are many, indeed. They extend from Sir Isaac Newton finding out about gravity in an orchard though he wasn't looking for it, to Sir Alexander Fleming spotting a mould, unwittingly, even carelessly left in a test-tube, while he was researching influenza. The ultimate outcome was the life-saving stuff we call penicillin.

Is this how God works, hiding beneficial treasures for us to trip over in his creation? And not only, maybe not mainly, of the materialistic, scientific kind? The unusually fine pearl the man in the other parable found is meant to represent something considerably more valuable than any literal pearl in the world. Joy, for instance, in the deepest sense.

And didn't C S Lewis testify that, when at last he was converted and became a Christian, he was *surprised by joy* ?

20

Pick up a stone

The Bible is littered with stones.   They speak to us. The idea of stones talking comes from Jesus. When he entered Jerusalem for the last time, riding his colt or donkey, the large crowd of his disciples and supporters gave him such a loud welcome that some of the religious officials ordered him to tell them to be quiet He replied: 'I tell you that if they keep quiet, the stones themselves will start shouting' (Luke 19: 40).

Shouting what? Many messages.

Pick up a stone and it will speak to you *of grateful memories.*

'So Jacob took a stone and set it up as a memorial.' That's in Genesis. Joshua did the same. So do we. When I ministered at Rodborough Tabernacle in the beautiful Cotswolds, I could walk around our church building and find many stones to remind me of the enormous debt we owe to our forefathers in the faith. Words in the Letter to the Hebrews quickly illuminate my mind like a Son et Lumiere. 'As for us,' the writer said, 'we have this large crowd of witnesses round us.' The memorials in the Tabernacle cry out for our gratitude. They recall the faith and witness of those who went before us in worship, prayer and dedicated service.

In the wake of the fiery trail George Whitefield left behind him there, a company of preachers met at the Tab every first Thursday to pray, plan their preaching missions across a wide area and dine together at the expense of one of their number, the aptly named Mr Hogg of Painswick.

Among them was William Vines, haymaking in the morning but with staff in hand walking to Bristol in the afternoon to preach. On a Sunday, another thirty-mile walk to a Wiltshire village to deliver a morning sermon; then more miles to another location for more preaching. Carrying his food in his pocket, he would stop to 'drink from the stream by the road', in the Psalmist's phrase, and eat his bread; and then, back to his regular job on Monday morning.

Also, there was Rowland Hill, son of a Shropshire baronet, surrendering home comforts and sacrificing his inheritance to be an itinerant preacher needing the selfsame Mr Hogg to rescue him from penury. These are two of many at the Tabernacle who went before us in the Way, proclaiming the Truth, living the Life. 'Should I go on?' asked the author of Hebrews. There wasn't enough time, he said, to speak of the many other witnesses. The same is true *of us*, as we view the memorials around us, reminders of the debt we owe wherever our church is located.

And are there not, in imagination at any rate, milestone memories for each of us personally along the way we've come? I often wonder what strangers, entering church as we sing a line like 'Here I raise my Ebenezer', would make of it. A cheap laugh? In their ignorance of scripture, those five words would seem incomprehensible nonsense; but there is something precious here, like a jeweller's stone. Ebenezer means 'Stone of Help'. Samuel set it up between Mizpah and Shen and said: 'The Lord has helped us all the way.' Don't we all feel a sense of gratitude that by the grace and mercy of God, we've come through thick and thin this far?

Pick up a stone, and it will warn us of *deadly weapons.*

Offenders were cruelly stoned to death in ancient Israel. The official procedure is too harrowing to be described here. But stones were also employed as weapons. The obvious case concerned David and Goliath, but how one justifies the story by claiming that God was with David as he felled poor old Goliath, I don't know. Not everything in the Bible is equally edifying.

Meditating on stones, I couldn't help recalling that old jingle about sticks and stones breaking our bones but words never hurting us. Such nonsense! Words do hurt, do break the spirit if not the bones.

A husband and wife went out to China as missionaries many years ago. Their little girl of six was left behind in a boarding school where a sadistic mistress made her life a misery. She longed for her parents to return home so that she could live with them. Eventually they were back. Meanwhile, however, they had had a baby boy on whom the mother doted. When mother and daughter met again, the mother said to her: 'Why, I'd almost forgotten I'd got you!' This careless remark inflicted so deep a wound on that young girl's personality that for ever afterwards she felt unwanted and unloved and in consequence had to receive psychotherapy. 'Almost without exception,' wrote William McDougall the psychologist 'children need to be encouraged in self-confidence rather than snubbed. And sometimes a single remark may have long-lasting effects.'

'A word rashly spoken,' says an old Chinese proverb, 'cannot be brought back by a chariot and four horses.' In Ecclesiastes one verse is sharply rendered 'Be not rash with thy mouth.' The Good News Bible renders verses in Proverbs like this: 'Kind words bring life, but cruel words crush your spirit.' And, of course, in the Letter of James chapter three, many verses are devoted to the dangers of an undisciplined, uncontrolled tongue. It is, writes James, a fire, a world of wrong, evil and full of deadly poison. Perhaps he suffered from unkind gossip!

Let the Psalmist's prayer ever be ours. 'Lord, place a guard at my mouth, a sentry at the door of my lips"

Pick up a stone, and it will remind us *of a despised Saviour who became a living Lord.*

That picture of a stone rejected as worthless by the builders but becoming the head-stone of the corner, the most important of all, is repeatedly presented to us in the Bible. It is a picture of Jesus who actually quotes the saying himself. It is applied to him. In a key Old Testament passage in Isaiah about the so-called Suffering Servant it says: 'We despised and rejected him.' He was disreputable, making himself of no reputation, as it says in the New Testament.

And he was crucified, the most ignominious death imaginable, and the cruellest. His rejection was complete. But his story wasn't. The work he had come to do was done on that cross, but he wasn't done for. He cried, 'It is finished.' That meant not that the grim ordeal of his suffering was over, but that his mission was 'accomplished'. He himself certainly wasn't 'finished'.

Which brings us to our last stone.

'On the way they said to one another, "Who will roll away the stone for us from the entrance to the tomb?" ' But, as Charles Wesley put it in his Easter hymn, 'Vain the stone, the watch, the seal.' Christ 'burst his three-day prison.' He ceased to be the despised and rejected Saviour and became the Lord who lives and leads. Someone said: 'The stone at the tomb of Jesus was a pebble to the Rock of Ages inside.' The stone once rejected becomes the Church's one foundation, and the Church as the Body of Christ continues his saving work in the world.

Easter, unlike Christmas, isn't a one-day festival, or even a twelve-day celebration, annually. Every Sunday is Easter Day. This year again, there were criticisms directed at shops and stores for marketing Easter goodies even before Christmas. One year, a correspondent wrote of seeing Easter eggs on sale in a Romford store, and the assistant explained: 'We thought they would make good stocking-fillers.' Another letter told of a superstore selling hot-cross buns on the Monday before Christmas.

Why not? These criticisms don't stand up. It is Easter that gives meaning to Christmas.

In Masefield's play *The Trial of Jesus*, Pilate's wife Procula is presented as being deeply troubled over the crucifixion of the preaching carpenter from Galilee. There is a base for scripture in this play, because Matthew tells us that she sent a message to her husband warning him not to have anything to do with Jesus, whom she described as an innocent man. A dream had troubled her. In the play she asks the Roman soldier who has rushed in to report an empty tomb, 'Where do you think he is?' He replies: 'Let loose in the world, lady, where neither Roman nor Jew can stop his truth.'

21

Instructing the cabin boy

The end of the book is 'happy ever after'. The story of Job, however, doesn't fit the kind of sentimental superficiality we find in Christmas pantomimes. Its theme is the dark problem of human suffering and injustice. The assumption that the colossal disaster which befalls Job must have been caused by his sin and wickedness doesn't tally with his exceptionally good character. The clear-cut theology that points to a God who punishes the evil person and benefits the righteous one is far too simple to be acceptable, especially in the light of our experience of life. Nevertheless, the book of Job, after all the anguish in its pages, does end happily.

Consider the tenth verse in the final chapter 42. In the Epilogue it says: 'The Lord restores the fortunes of Job, when he had prayed for his friends; and the Lord gave Job twice as much as he had before.'

On the surface it sounds rather mercenary. Job prayed for his friends, and it was he who benefitted. Double your income by intercession! It pays to pray. If such an idea really worked and it caught on, we would be corrupted, and worshippers not of the God and Father (and Mother) of our Lord Jesus Christ, but of the golden idol of self-interest.

There are pulpits, more in America than here, where the incumbent preaches the profitability of faith in sheer material terms, where God's favour is seen in worldly success and prosperity. In the twelfth verse of chapter 42, it says that Job received in grossly inflated figures, 'fourteen thousand sheep and six thousand camels, a thousand yoke of oxen, and as many she-donkeys'. This, of course, is *hyperbole*, 'an exaggerated statement not meant to be taken literally'

We reflect that the prayers of Jesus before and after Gethsemane didn't exactly bring him any earthly prosperity. He suffered and died on a cross, his cloak was divided among the on-looking soldiers and his broken body was laid to rest in a borrowed grave. The profit motive for prayer is out, and we know this in our hearts only too well.

I move from Job and Jesus to John Wesley. I open his Journal at an entry early in 1738. He was limping through a personal crisis just then. He was engaged on a Christian mission in Georgia. He admitted that he had embarked on the project to save his own soul more than to save others, By preaching the gospel to the heathen, he thought that he would solve his own spiritual problems. It didn't work out that way: it never does. These were the dark days before Wesley had become a soundly converted and completely convinced Christian.

To add to his troubles, he had passed through a disappointing courtship which ended in a broken engagement. We pick up the story in his Journal as he set sail for England, the abortive American trip over.He was a thoroughly depressed and dejected man. He wrote on 2nd January 1738 of 'being sorrowful and very heavy, though I could give no particular reason for it, and utterly unwilling to speak close to any of my little flock (about twenty persons), I was in doubt whether my neglect of them was not one cause of my own heaviness.' Then comes the most telling entry in this part of his Journal. Wesley writes: 'In the evening therefore I began *instructing the cabin* boy; after which I was much easier.'

How significant are those sixteen words! Picture the scene. Wesley sunk in gloom, his attention turned entirely inwards. But once he finds someone to take himself out of himself, the fog lying on his soul lifts and the sun breaks through. He forgets himself, gives his mind afresh to his life's mission in declaring the loving purpose of God, and with that upward and outward look, he finds healing for his ailing spirit.

A basic rule for right living lies in Job praying for his friends, and John Wesley instructing the cabin boy. We are made by God to spend more time looking upward and outward than inward.

Inner serenity and happiness, the two fond desires of all human beings, come to us in small or large measure in accordance with our willingness to keep a balance among these three: inward, outward and upward. Failure here, and an undue self-regard with God and others blotted out, is a direct and dangerous denial of what it means by God's own plan to be human.

I came across an old parable not long ago. It is a parable of care.

> Once when "Care" was crossing a river, she saw some clay. She thoughtfully took up a piece and began to shape it. While she was meditating on what she had made, Jupiter came by. "Care" asked him to give it spirit, and this he gladly granted. But when she wanted her name to be bestowed upon it, he forbade this, and demanded that it be given his name instead.
>
> While "Care" and Jupiter were disputing, Earth arose and desired that her own name be conferred on the creature, since she had furnished it with part of her body. They asked Saturn to be their arbiter, and he made the following decision which seemed a just one: "Since you, Jupiter, have given it spirit you shall receive that spirit at its death; and since you, Earth, have given it a body, you shall receive its body. But since "Care" first shaped this creature, she shall possess it as long as it lives. And because there is now a dispute among you as to its name, let it be called "homo" for it is made out of "humus" – earth."

So ends the parable. Its interpretation is that the capacity to care is the meaning of being human.

Concern for others is God's intention, it seems, for every one of us. If we stifle that God-given capacity, do we not become less than human and lose hope of fulfilling our lives as God intends?

William Blake wrote a poem about a little man standing at the foot of a great ladder. It reaches up into the clouds. There he is, standing with arms outstretched and head thrown back and shouting, 'I want! I want! It is a picture of the person who lives only for self-satisfaction. There is no end to the ladder. The more he wants, the less he finds; the more he does what he likes, the less he likes what he does. A New York newspaper reporter wrote... 'Broadway is full of amusement places trying to make people happy by appealing to their every human instinct, yet so many of its people are drenched in unhappiness.' They don't listen to Job, don't want to know about John Wesley, don't care to hear about Jesus. The inward lookers!

Here is a sorry paradox. The religion that <u>goes</u> by the precious name of Jesus Christ is meant to be totally altruistic. So much of our religious faith and practice, however, is self-centred. 'And there will be,' says the old hymn, *'glory for me.'*

I visited a home where its two occupants told me that they weren't so sure of God any more. I heard how they had been confronted by a number of vexing but comparatively minor domestic difficulties. They told me that they had always faithfully prayed to God and he had always faithfully answered their prayers. Now, sad to say, he had apparently been letting them down; and now they doubted him, his goodness and his love. They couldn't see the utter self-centredness of their whole approach to God and prayer.

When Lord MacLeod of Fuinary was Dr George MacLeod, minister of the Presbyterian Church of Scotland, he wrote an impressive book entitled *Only One Way Left.* Early in its pages, he warned us against making religion a kind of hobby for sheer self-satisfaction. 'The real trouble,' he wrote, 'is that the Bible is not about that sort of religion at all. In the Bible God is a total Sovereign not a personal solace. Authentic solace resides in a serious acceptance of his total sovereignty. God is at the hub round which the whole wheel of life revolves. If we make of him a spiritual hobby, we end by creating him in our own image.'

Thinking of these things, I find myself faced with searching questions.

What is my motive for praying, churchgoing and giving practical service?

Is my faith really directed upwards and outwards, or is it a kind of spiritual insurance policy to get me to heaven?

Do I set out to glorify and serve God, or merely to use him?

Am I attempting to save my own soul in the service I render to others?

22

Jesus Christ Troubadour

Did Jesus <u>sing</u>, hymns? Almost certainly he did. Two of the Gospels tell us about the ending of the Last Supper by saying, 'Then they sang a hymn and went out to the Mount of Olives.' If that Supper was, in fact, the Passover meal, that hymn would have been the Great Hallel, the thanksgiving for God's goodness and eternal love in Psalm 136. It chronicles the deliverance of the Children of Israel from Egypt and ultimately into the Promised Land. Hallel as in Hallelujah.

Jesus surely joined in that final Passover hymn. Was he tenor, baritone or bass? No matter. But as I thought of a singing Jesus, I recollected a visit we paid to the Theatre Royal, Stratford East to see *The Singer*, a jazz musical performed by a company of talented amateurs. Based on a book by Calvin Miller, an American Baptist pastor, the show retold the gospel story as if St John had begun his Gospel with the words: 'In the beginning was the Song....' The musical could have been sub-titled *Jesus Christ Troubadour*. It portrayed Jesus, guitar in hand, offering the world his song of love. It ended with the message 'Go ye into all the world and sing the song.'

From time immemorial, religion has found its expression in music and song and hymn. There are musical details in some of the stories and sayings associated with Jesus. When the Prodigal is welcomed home, there is music and dancing. When Jesus compares his ministry with that of John the Baptist he talks about children sitting in the market place and calling to each other... 'We played wedding music for you, but you wouldn't dance! We sang funeral songs to you, but you wouldn't cry!' (Luke 7: 32) Luke has the birth of Jesus announced by an angelic choir: *Gloria in Excelsis Deo*. It is Luke who gives us those other hymns, for such they are: the Magnificat, the Benedictus and the Nunc Dimmitis.

Jesus Christ has profoundly influenced the world of music over the centuries. Remove all works relating to the life, passion, death and resurrection of Jesus from two millennia of musical composition and performance, and what have we left? An enormous gap, a major loss. In a Festival Sermon in Lichfield Cathedral, Dr Gordon Wakefield said, 'The very name of Jesus is music, "music in the sinner's ears".' That phrase comes, of course, from Charles Wesley's 'O for a thousand tongues to sing my great Redeemer's praise', and John Newton added, 'And may the music of Thy name refresh my soul in death.'

In our Free Church tradition, the voice and sentiments of the congregation find their main expression through the hymns. They are not intended merely to give us the chance to stand up and have 'a good sing'. Through them we speak to God, pray to him, praise and adore him. Many if not most hymns are prayers. It is essential that the words and phrases given us by the hymnodists are right and natural for us to use as we address and applaud God.

Albert van den Heuvel, the radical and outspoken Dutch church leader, believed in hymns as the container of our faith. He complained that while our task was to work for an urban faith, we still sang on Sundays about nothing but nature. We now have hymns, at least in quality hymn books like *Rejoice and Sing*, enabling us to articulate mind and feeling to God in words and phrases more natural to us. Our great hymnody pioneer Erik Routley used to say that a hymn has done its work when the worshipper can feel 'This is what I wanted to say, but I am grateful to whoever put the words in my mouth.'

In his book *The Use of Hymns*, Canon Alan Dunstan refers to those down the Christian centuries 'who saw hymnody as a direct method of teaching doctrine'. John Wesley, for example. Early on in the Methodist movement, in 1780, he wrote of their first collection of hymns: 'It is large enough to contain all the important truths of our most holy religion ... so that this book is, in effect, a little body of experimental and practical divinity.' Canon Dunstan comments: 'Hymns have been peculiarly valued in the Methodist Church, not only because of the high place that they have held in its liturgy and in the private devotion of its members, but because the hymn book has been seen as a manual of doctrine. When a Methodist theologian expounds a doctrine, it is not long before he starts quoting a hymn.'

So hymns have a doctrinal purpose. The best of them teach and instruct us in the things of God as revealed to us through Jesus Christ. In the New Testament church, so far as we can make out, the songs the first Christians introduced into the fellowship formed the basis of the creeds later to be set out to defend the faith against heresy and the hostile attacks from its enemies. Such teaching isn't the only purpose and value of a good hymn, but it's an important one.

Down in the pew, we tend to shy away from terms like doctrine and theology. In our Free Church tradition, we find distaste in a word like 'indoctrinate' and we fear theologians for allegedly complicating what we call the 'simple' gospel, and even for shaking our faith. Denis Diderot, the eighteenth-century sceptic, complained: 'I have only a small flickering light to guide me in the darkness of a thick forest. Up comes a theologian and blows it out.'

It ill behoves us to scorn theologies and their exponents. We need doctrinal instruction to keep us on the strait and narrow path of orthodox belief in a sceptical and oft-times cynical secular world. Furthermore, such teaching isn't obscure speculation meant only for arguing over by dons in their ivory towers. Colin Morris has rightly reminded us that 'theology is what you are when the talking stops and the action starts.'

Next time I go to church I will take care to listen more intently for the Word of God in the words chosen that day for us all to sing. In *Sing With The Understanding*, G R Balleine warns us not to resemble the

> *Two little birds in a wood*
> *Who sang hymns whenever they could*
> *What the words were about*
> *They could never make out;*
> *But they thought that it did them some good*

Such woolly vagueness is no way to regard and sing the doctrinal hymns.

By way of hymns we seek God in trouble and in joy through all the changing scenes of life. As well as engaging the mind, a good hymn will stir the heart. It will appeal to feelings as well as to the intellect. There are hymns for all seasons and circumstances.

James in his Letter asks, 'Is anyone happy?' and then says, 'He should sing praises.'   Let us rejoice and sing, for as C S Lewis affirmed, 'Joy is the serious business of heaven.' But what if life deals us one of its harsh blows and we are brought low? Can God's praises employ heart and tongue then, when the scene changes and we are in trouble?

How about Paul and Silas, arrested in Philippi because those with vested interests found that these two were harmful to their business. The missionaries were divested of their clothes, severely beaten and thrown into gaol with their feet fastened into stocks. Despite their suffering and confinement we read that 'about midnight Paul and Silas were praying and singing hymns to God, and the other prisoners were listening to them.' (Acts 16: 25) Such is the power of Christian witness in adversity, expressed through hymns. That situation and the Christian response to it have been repeated many times through history. A seventeenth-century Quaker Williaim Dewsbury left us his testimony. 'In the prison house I sang praises to my God,' he said, 'and esteemed the bolts and locks put upon me as jewels'

Thanks be to God for our hymns. Through them we address and applaud God whose saving Word comes through them to us in trouble and in joy. And Jesus surely sang hymns, even as he sang one just before going out to the Mount of Olives on that fateful night long ago.

23

The Clown of Sorrows

Every so often, the thirteenth of the month falls on a Friday, as in February and August 2004 and in May 2005.

We all know what folklore says about the number thirteen. It betokens bad luck. I read that the Turkish people so detest the number that it is virtually expunged from their vocabulary. The Italians won't use it in their lotteries. In Paris, no house bears the number. In America too.

Martin Luther King, in one of his impressive sermons, talked about those soft-minded individuals whose superstitious minds are constantly invaded by irrational fears such as the fear of Friday the thirteenth. Once he was ascending in a large New York hotel elevator. He noticed that there was no thirteenth floor. The elevator went from twelve to fourteen. He asked the operator, the lift man, why. 'This practice is followed by most large hotels,' the man explained, 'because of the fear of numerous people to stay on a thirteenth floor.' Then he added, 'The real foolishness of the fear is to be found in the fact that the fourteenth floor is actually the thirteenth.'

More than forty years ago when I was pastor of a small village church, Margaret told me that one member of the Women's Meeting had gone home before the proceedings had begun because upon her arrival there were twelve present, and she would have made thirteen.

In Christian countries that superstition is based on the belief that the Last Supper was unlucky because there were thirteen present. In high Parisian society there were people known as *Quatorziennes*. They were professional guests who stood in readiness to join a party in case it turned out otherwise to be thirteen strong.

So, thirteen is widely regarded in folklore to be an unlucky number. And Friday, whether thirteenth or not is likewise felt to be an unlucky day. In Anglo-Saxon times they used to say that Adam and Eve ate the forbidden fruit on a Friday and died on a Friday. And, of course, Jesus was crucified on a Friday. A bad day, the worst of all in history, to be sure. The ancient Romans dubbed Friday *nefastus*, meaning unlucky, ill-omened, because their entire army was totally overthrown at Gallia Narbonensis on that day. That was nothing compared with the crucifixion of the Son of God on a green hill far away around AD 33.

Folklore, mind you, views Good Friday as good as well as bad. The Scots, I believe, look upon it as a good day for weddings. In the Greek Church it is known as Great Friday because a great salvation was won for humankind in some deeply mysterious way by that Man, Son of God and Saviour. Racine, the French dramatist, has a character who says, 'He who laughs on Friday will weep on Sunday.' For Christian people, the exact opposite is the case.

Every so often, Good Friday also coincides with April Fools' Day.

In the Middle Ages the jesters engaged to amuse the king obtained their jokes and stories from various jest books in circulation, much as modem comedians rely on their script-writers. One story in circulation told of a friar who rebuked his congregation for going off riding on a Sunday. He directed his gaze as he spoke towards one man who was all ready to ride, his boots and spurs on. The mediaeval joke book said: 'This man, perceiving that all the people noted him, suddenly half in anger answered the friar thus: "Why preachest ye so much against them that ride on the Sunday? For Christ himself did ride on Psalm Sunday. As thou knowest well, it is written in Holy Scripture." To whom the friar suddenly answered and said thus, "But I pray ye, what came thereof? Was he not hanged on the Friday after?" ' And the story ends by telling us that when they heard this, "all the people in the church fell on laughing".

We wouldn't. We would think this tale lacking in taste. Laughing at a crude reference to Jesus on his cross. How could they? And how can our minister begin his sermon on Good Friday by repeating it? The answer is that Jesus was laughed at unmercifully just before and during his crucifixion. The jesters' joke is nothing compared with the mockery Jesus endured as they prepared him for his cross, and actually as he hung there. The Roman soldiery, the watching crowd, the religious leaders, even the criminals crucified with him all joined in. They turned him into a clown, a figure of fun, a fool to be laughed at.

There is an early tradition in the Church that sees Christ as a clown. It has been revived in our time, and there is a biblical basis for it. The American theologian Harvey Cox compares Jesus to a wandering troubadour, a minstrel frequenting dinners and parties, a man costumed by his enemies in a mocking caricature of royal paraphernalia. 'He is crucified amidst sniggers and taunts,' Dr Cox reminds us, 'with a sign over his head that lampoons his laughable claim.'

Somewhat fanciful, far-fetched, even offensive, you might say. Some do not take easily or kindly to the figure of Christ the clown, any more than they care for the poetic portrayal of the Lord of the Dance. But then, who can sit contentedly with the idea of a crucified Saviour? Paul, addressing the Corinthians, declared that 'we proclaim the crucified Christ a message that is offensive to the Jews and nonsense to the Gentiles' (1 Corinthians 1: 23). The Lord of creation was ready, out of love for us, to be made foolish, to appear as a clown, a buffoon, a knockabout, for us and for our salvation. There is the 'folly of the Cross'.

Good Friday, as I say, sometimes falls on April Fools' Day. Not inappropriately. The custom of such a day combined with the day commemorating the execution of Jesus leads some church historians to suppose that the 'April fool' tricks and stunts are based on the mockery of Jesus, the Clown of Sorrows.

Clowns aren't flippant figures. There is a sadness surrounding them. The great clowns of circus, theatre and film have made us laugh, but there is a pathos about them. Charlie Chaplin and Buster Keaton are prime examples; and we always felt sorry, too, for Laurel and Hardy. We laugh till the tears run down our faces. Tears! Our comic geniuses are prepared to make fools of themselves, but beneath their masks of fun there lurks the suspicion of an aching heart for real, or put on as part of the act. Norman Wisdom sings 'Don't laugh at me 'cos I'm a fool.' Ken Dodd's 'happiness' song is matched in his repertoire with another about tears. We are familiar with the notion that a clown's comic make-up and costume may hide a deep unhappiness. The tradition of the brokenhearted clown remains. Gilbert and Sullivan gave us the apt example of it in Jack Point the jester, dying for his unrequited love of a lady in *The Yeoman of the Guard*.

Clowns have been introduced into church services over the years. The most impressive instance of this occurred in America. I received a letter from a United Reformed Church minister who crossed the Atlantic to serve as pastor of a New Jersey congregation, and he told me what had happened.

One Sunday morning, immediately before sharing in the Lord's Supper, they showed the film *Parable* which presents a Jesus-figure as a white-faced clown in a travelling circus. He was the odd man out reacting to the vicissitudes of life patiently, passively and differently from others. He was what Americans call the 'fall guy' in every situation.

A young woman in that congregation who was a drama student secretly made herself up exactly as the clown in the film. As the communicants were clustering around the Table, she walked in from the main vestibule in complete silence. They couldn't tell who she was. She came to the Table and stood there with the two officiating ministers. As they spoke the words of the Institution, so the clown broke the bread and lifted the cup. At the blessing at the end, so my correspondent wrote, the clown slipped quietly away and was not seen again. The letter said that it was a 'fantastic experience' for all of them.

I should add that our brilliant hymnodist Brian Wren wrote some verses which must have been inspired by that haunting and enigmatic film *Parable*. They appear in *Rejoice and Sing* at number 225, and their author, portraying the Christ as a 'discarded scarecrow' asks the question:

> *Can such a clown of sorrows*
> *still bring a useful word*
> *where faith and love seem phantoms*
> *and every hope absurd?*

24

The flowers that bloom in the spring

A poem by Steve Turner satirically suggests that what happened at Passiontide and Easter isn't good for nervous people. It includes whips, blood, nails, a spear and 'allegations of body snatching'. It involves politics, God and the sins of the world. Better for the nervous to think about the coming of spring and its first dewdrop, about rabbits, chickens, and cream-filled eggs.

The trouble is that Easter, the major Christian festival, is historically intertwined with the pagan festival of spring. The very word Easter comes from 'Eostre' the spring goddess The celebrations we observe at Christmas are similarly mixed up with the Roman Saturnalia and the northern Yuletide, although the red-robed, white-bearded Father Christmas derives from a fourth century, mid-eastern bishop. With his reindeer, sleigh and sacks of toys, he was introduced into western culture from Germany as late as 1840.

At Easter, instead of praising God for raising his Son our Saviour Jesus Christ from the dead, we may catch ourselves getting lyrical and even sentimental over Wordsworth's host of golden daffodils, fluttering and dancing in the breeze. John in his Gospel tells us that the new tomb in which they tenderly laid the broken body of Jesus was located in a garden. What we spotlight at Easter isn't the garden but the tomb emptied of its body because God had raised Jesus. As W S Gilbert, writing *The Mikado* more than a century ago, would remark, the flowers that bloom in the spring tra la, have nothing to do with the case.

Last Christmas, we received as usual a round-robin from our American friends retired in North Carolina. Now well into their eighties and still actively youthful, they wrote: 'Santa Claus, Christmas trees and poinsettias have nothing to do with God's gift to us of the Prince of Peace in a tiny baby.'

When Paul on his missionary travels reached Athens, he met with his toughest audience. Ever probing, posing questions and engaging in intellectual exercise and debate, they failed as much as he did. He couldn't get through to them, and they didn't cotton on to him. They were quite unable to grasp his message about Jesus and the Resurrection, so we are told in Acts 17: 18. 'He would appear to be a propagandist for foreign deities,' they muttered.

In passing, we note that 'propagandist' is the word used in both the The Revised English Bible and the Jerusalem Bible. It is a word which reminds people of my generation of the Nazis, especially Joseph Goebbels. The Church of Rome has its *congregatio de propaganda fide* – the congregation for the propagation of the faith. The word itself means, the dictionary informs us, 'an organized programme of publicity'.

Another interesting point here is that those argumentative egg-heads of Athens would have heard Paul use their own Greek word for 'resurrection' which, in its feminine form, gives us the name 'Anastasia'. Did they think that he was referring to some goddess probably of nature? There were many such in the ancient Graeco-Roman pantheon. That word means 'many gods'. Was this visiting philosopher Paul, as they saw him, simply adding another god to the list?

As if to correct the impression that he was in the nature deity business, Paul, in his address to the city council, made it clear that the one and only God was the Maker and Lord of heaven and earth and everything in the world. This God, Paul went on, has proved himself by raising Jesus from the dead. It was the Resurrection that Paul preached, not a panegyric to nature.

But, you will protest, isn't nature part of the total picture? Isn't the springtime an admirable illustration of new life bursting forth from death? The daffodils spring up in April out of a dead earth. Yes, of course; and every Eastertide we sing those sentiments of John of Damascus from twelve centuries past:

> 'Tis the Spring of souls today,
> Christ hath burst His prison,
> And from three days 'sleep in death
> As the sun hath risen;

All the winter of our sins,
Long and dark is flying
From His light, to Whom we give
Laud and praise undying.

Such is the translation by John Mason Neale of some verses by John of Damascus.

The poets and hymn-writers often use nature as an *illustration of* resurrection, but an illustration only. What happens in the natural world points to the mighty Easter event.

If Jesus died, naught but the winter and the gloom remain
But Jesus lives!
Then full and fain, laugh and sing ye golden flowers,
Drifting clouds and dancing showers,
Christ is risen! Christ is risen!
God's green Spring is true again.

To <u>illustrate</u> the Resurrection: that's the point. For there is danger here. Hubert Van Zeller said: 'Looked at in the wrong way, nature can be a substitute for God.'

Nature, as we well know, is all very beautiful but it has its ugly face too. Yes, God is good, cries the hymn; and ten thousand voices seem to cry, 'God made us all, and God is good.' But ten thousand other voices from ocean depths and spreading wood tell of another less welcome truth. There are sharks with jaws, giant destructive waves, and greenfly to ruin your garden; for nature is red in tooth and claw. You will have heard 'The Gardener's Hymn', a parody of 'All things bright and beautiful.' It mentions 'The fungus on the goose-gogs, the club root on the greens, the slugs that eat the lettuce and chew the aubergines.' There is also 'the draught that kills the fuchsias, the frost that nips the buds, the rain that drowns the seedlings, the blight that hits the spuds'.

Nature is a rather wild instrument through which God the Creator operates, but God isn't to be equated with nature.

I value my green-covered copy of *Daily Readings from William Temple* published in 1948. The finest and wisest writing never dates. 'In nature we find God,' wrote Temple, ...'Yet the self-revelation so given is incomplete and inadequate. Personality can only reveal itself in persons. Consequently it is specially in Human Nature – in men and women – that we see God.' And, we must add, it is in beholding the Man Jesus, crucified and risen, that we see God and discern his loving purpose most clearly.

Easter is, therefore, the time to celebrate the living Christ and to expound the theme of life. It is, moreover, an all-the-year-round festival. It was R W Dale of Birmingham, the distinguished minister of Carr's Lane Congregational Church in the latter part of the nineteenth century, who insisted that an Easter hymn be included in every morning service that he conducted. This demand arose out of an experience he had while writing an Easter sermon. Halfway through, the thought of the Risen Christ broke in on him as never before. Instinctively, Dale was right. Every Sunday is an Easter Day. Easter is an evergreen, whereas spring comes and goes and occupies but a quarter of the year. Robert Herrick is forced to cry out:

> Fair daffodils, we weep to see
> You haste away so soon.

And spring isn't reliable either. It isn't all sunshine. There can be chill winds, heavy rain, even sleet. One Easter Sunday morning, I remember hearing on the radio that it was raining in Jerusalem. On another long ago, as I recall, I drove through snow to conduct a service in Suffolk.

Nevertheless, whatever the outward conditions, the bright light of the Easter message remains and illuminates us every week and every day, for Christ is risen and is alive for evermore.

25
Not for sale

I walked into a shop in modern Jerusalem where among the goods on display were tins of fresh air collected in all seriousness among the rocks of the Judaean wilderness. Visitors bought these tins and took them home to America or wherever in the world they lived. Is there no end to the follies of humankind? Thank God that there are some things which are not for sale.

Not for sale! The phrase leads me to First Kings 21, and to Naboth's Vineyard. It adjoined the palace of King Ahab of Samaria. Ahab saw the possibility of turning it into a private garden for the royal court, and he made Naboth an offer: a better vineyard in exchange, or a straight financial deal. Naboth turned the offer down. The property had been in his family for generations, and it is likely that some of his ancestors were buried there. Anyway, Israel had a tradition that one simply didn't barter one's inheritance, a grave sin that Esau had committed in the distant past. Naboth said in effect, 'Not for sale.'

It cost him his life. Ahab fell into an angry sulk, took to his bed and went on hunger strike. Jezebel, the king's scheming wife, arranged for Naboth to be followed, framed and judicially murdered. He was unjustly accused and died by stoning. He paid dearly for his loyalty to the principle that there are some things in life that aren't for sale.

Clearing up a home after a loved one has died can be a melancholy experience. A sorting operation gets under way, and you have four boxes bearing their respective labels: one for the fire, one for your friends, one for the shop. For the saving of those items to be kept for sentimental reasons, the fourth box will be labelled NOT FOR SALE.

Love is not for sale. Sex may be, but that's another story.

Henry Ward Beecher, an American preacher so famed in his day that a clever limerick was made up about him, was out walking with a member of his congregation. They passed the home of an exceptionally wealthy man. 'Ah that's old So-and so's house,' remarked the other man. 'Why should he be rolling in riches, while I have to struggle along on 20 dollars a week?'

Beecher just then made no comment, but instead of parting at the corner they walked on till they reached Beecher's friend's home. They went indoors. There, waiting, was the man's wife and his children. The preacher picked up John, one of the children. John's mother said, 'I wouldn't sell him for his weight in gold.' Beecher replied, 'By the feel of him, I'd say he weighs about 40lbs. That's about ten thousand dollars. But it would be the same if it were ten million, wouldn't it?' Then Beecher turned to John's father and said, 'Old So-and-so hasn't a child or a wife like yours. And you said, "Why should he be rolling in riches?" '

Our ties of love do not belong to the realm of commercial transaction. They are so precious they cannot be priced, can never be for sale. When the Epworth Rectory went up in flames at midnight on 9th February 1709, the young John Wesley became 'a brand plucked from the burning'. He was narrowly rescued. His father cried out, 'Let us give thanks to God. He has given me all my eight children. Let the house go!' That meant all Samuel Wesley's books, papers, paintings and sermons, It takes some doing to watch a lifetime's work go up in flames,

Preachers are often anxious about their sermon scripts. If there is a fire in the manse they say that the first thing a minister will do is to carry his priceless sermons to safety. But that's just a joke. He or she will first ensure that loved ones are safe. The wonderful fact is that love is not for sale.

Faith is not for sale. It isn't a negotiable commodity.

Among the *dramatis personae* in the Book of Acts we come across Simon the sorcerer in the eighth chapter. He lived in Samaria and had impressed people with his supposedly magical powers. He was possibly a kind of first-century amalgam of the two Pauls, Daniels and McKenna. He performed tricks, created illusions before their very eyes and undoubtedly scooped in a handsome living. Credulous spectators thought that he was endowed with special powers, and some of them even hailed him as divine.

He belonged to a class of astrologers, soothsayers and magicians commonly encountered in those days. Not that we need be scornfully superior about such as Simon. There is widespread belief in fortune-telling and star-gazing today, with a pathetic regard to star-signs. There are plenty of smart opportunists in our society who make money out of these dubious beliefs.

Simon is mentioned in the New Testament because he became a Christian. He wasn't content however, to be, as we might say, an ordinary Christian. He had noticed that the apostles Peter and John by the laying on of hands bestowed the gift of the Holy Spirit on their converts in Samaria. Thinking no doubt that such a facility might prove useful as an addition to his bag of tricks, and assuming that the gift could be bought over the counter, he offered cash for it. Peter gave him an angry dressing down. 'You thought God's gift was for sale? Your money can go with you to damnation!'

The corrupt practice of buying one's way into high ecclesiastical office, particularly prevalent in the fourth century, became known as 'simony'.

Faith, and all that faith means, cannot be traded with. 'The gospel,' wrote Murdo Ewan Macdonald, 'is not something ready-made, neatly packaged, handed down from the shelf of tradition to any customer who might come along.' The apostle Paul wrote of 'my gospel' meaning the gospel of Christ worked out in his own life and made his own. In a sense, every person's gospel is different. Faith is not for sale in identical packets.

Heaven is not for sale. It is by grace that we are saved through faith.

The idea persists that a person can amass enough currency to obtain a plot in heaven, to stake a claim upon God for a place in the next life. Such currency is usually conceived in terms of good deeds. Do enough good works, and you'll get in. How can he up there refuse you if you show him your good-deed bank account?

This is a heresy from former generations, and it puts our relationship with God on the totally wrong footing. Austin Farrer, Christian scholar and thinker, once wrote: 'Heaven is not a cash payment for walking with God, it is where the road goes.' It isn't something you obtain in exchange for a fat cheque, like a widescreen TV set, or a sports car, or six months in the Bahamas. C S Lewis said that 'Heaven offers nothing that a mercenary soul can desire,'

It is by amazing grace that salvation is granted to us. It is a free gift. God doesn't charge us for it, any more than you would charge your son and daughter for the love you give them. Imagine asking young John or Mary for 5p of their weekly pocket money for a little affection for the coming week. The very notion revolts us, as well it may. So it is with God's grace and the gift of heaven, a gift available now, and not exclusively after this life's ending.

Fulton Sheen was a glamorous American bishop who courted the media and became a TV personality. 'The only things we can carry with us at death,' he said, 'are what we might carry away in a shipwreck,'

Let me pause for thought, and ponder what this means. We can take nothing saleable; nothing tied up with the tinkle of the bell on the cash register. We can take only the things of the heart like love, faith, friendship, goodwill, hope, joy, peace.

Let me cultivate these while I live in this world. Of what real and ultimate worth is all the rest?

26

Breaking ice and dawning light

People of my generation will remember Dr Ian Ramsey, Bishop of Durham. Among my papers I have some record of an impressive utterance he delivered at a BBC meeting three weeks before he died. He spoke about revelation, about the way in which you and I come to a knowledge of the truth. There are two contrasting ways, he pointed out, whereby the process of revelation may occur. He labelled them with a pair of striking metaphors: *the ice breaks* and *the light dawns*.

Above the delectable West Riding town of Ilkley on the edge of the moor, the Tarn is something between a large pond and a small lake. The hope, especially among the local young, is for a chilly winter to bring snow and enough ice to freeze the Tarn hard enough for skating. Although we spent seven years in the town, I was too sleekit, cow'rin and tim'rous a beastie, like the Robert Burns mouse, to launch myself on to the unreliable ice.

In the annals of Sudbury, our nearest town in Suffolk, our retirement county, we have our river Stour, which has been known to freeze over. My wife Margaret's paternal grandmother in her Victorian schooldays was known to have skated to school on the Stour. The river must have frozen over during the winter of 1789 which inflicted a severe frost, for a month from mid-December, upon the town. The Thames that year certainly froze to a depth of eighteen feet at Blackfriars.

Breaking ice is a fearful phenomenon. To have it crack and crumble beneath one's weight and to be suddenly plunged into the exceedingly cold water beneath must be a horrible experience. It may be a huge joke in funny films or fiction, but in real life it is an unpleasant shock-making mishap.

The moment of truth may be equally sudden and similarly unpleasant. The process of conversion may be an ice-breaking experience. Church history chronicles such sudden changes in the lives of many. The consequences may be altogether good, but the flashing blow causing the change may well be stunning and painful. Like, as I say, an instant plunge into icy water.

Or like the birth of a child. John Wesley saw it thus. He preached about the second birth, the mark of Christian conversion, as being like our first and natural birth. 'When that strange, mysterious downward thrust forces the child into life,' he said, '.... it is sudden.' It is what Jesus hints at in his conversation in the quiet cool of the night with Nicodemus. 'I am telling you the truth: no one can see the Kingdom of God unless he is born again'. (John 3: 3)

From breaking ice we turn to the dawning light. This, too, is an illustration of another way whereby revelation comes to us.

I recall a visit in my youth to our local Palace Theatre to see *Old Chelsea*, a musical show in which we expected to see Richard Tauber. As it was, we didn't. He was confined to a Reading hotel with bronchitis, and his understudy played the part.

The show portrayed eighteenth-century London with bright sets and costumes. One scene fixed itself in my memory mainly because of the special lighting effects. It showed the dawn gradually creeping over the darkened sky and rooftops of old Chelsea. The orchestra played a piece of background music to enhance the total effect.

If in these days I wake up too early to get up I stay awake (if I can!) and watch the morning light through the bedroom window coming upon us, so gradually yet inevitably. In the show, slowly though more quickly than in nature, daylight spread its warm glow over the entire stage setting. Till, in fact, the whole scene came alive with the bright light of a summer morning.

In just such a way the truth dawns upon our darkened minds. It is a gradual process. It happens quietly and without our being aware of it. We grow into faith by an unobtrusive, continuous unfolding of the truth. It must be so, for the truth in its totality is so vast and profound that you and I cannot possibly take it into our systems all at once. We shall gradually awaken to it over many years. Jesus was fully aware of this. In that Upper Room, as he spoke to his men for the last time on earth, he told them that he hadn't told them everything. 'I have much more to tell you,' he declared, 'but now it would be too much for you to bear.' He went on to promise them the dawning light. 'When, however, the Spirit comes, who reveals the truth about God, he will lead you into all the truth.' (John 16: 12-13)

These, then, are two ways in which revelation occurs. The ice breaks, the light dawns.

Paradoxically, both are true together. We see God suddenly, we catch sight of his face slowly.

It happens likewise in the relationship of love between human beings. Canon Bryan Green of Birmingham used to remind his congregation that conversion to Christ and the Christian way was rather like falling in love. It could be a sudden emotional experience, happening at a definite time and in a particular place. In later years husband and wife may well return to the precise spot and celebrate the event on the very anniversary day.

There is such a thing as love at first sight. This heady phenomenon has been regularly presented on stage and screen and in novels. In South Pacific the romantic Frenchman sings of some enchanted evening when you see your true love across a crowded room. But there is also gradual love. It is a slow-growing relationship, possibly a longstanding family friendship slipping into an experience of love. As with human ties, so with men and women in their knowledge of God. The ice breaks, the light dawns.

There may be many genuine and sincere followers of Jesus Christ within our churches who, sure enough of their faith, are yet troubled because they cannot look back to a specific conversion experience at a precise location on some Damascus Road. I say to them, 'Worry ye not!' We need to be born again, but this spiritual rebirth doesn't have to be a sudden, dramatic happening.

In *The Devil's Advocate*, a novel by Morris West, there was Nerone, the deserter who became a saint. In his diary he wrote of how he moved from doubt to faith. He groped for God but couldn't find him. He prayed to God without getting an answer. There were tears. Then God was there. Nerone should have been able to give the time, the place and the manner of it. He should have been able to say that he believed when he saw creation in the face of a child. It wasn't like that at all. 'There are no words to record,' he said, 'no stones scored with a fiery finger, no thunders on Tabor. I had a Father and He knew me and the world was a house that He had built for me.'

The breaking of the ice, let it be said, doesn't mean an arrival rather than a beginning. None of us has arrived: we are pilgrims on the road. There can be no cosy settling back to bask in the comforts of the Kingdom when there is so much to learn of God, so many creases to iron out of our own sinful natures, so widespread a need in the world for Christian action and service.

I have read somewhere that there are two different kinds of ideal. There are *authentic* ideals, and *phantom* ideals. The authentic leads to action. A person entertains a high and pure vision of a just society. Not simply basking in the warm glow of that vision, he or she goes out and in every practical way open to them they toil and strive to translate that ideal into reality. The phantom ideal, as psychiatrist Anthony Storr defined it, is something which arouses our ardour without affecting our behaviour. Somebody entertains a vision of a just society, and that's all they do: entertain it. To sit in a pew each week, share in a service and even enjoy a good sermon can be little different from sitting in a cinema seat watching an edifying film and enjoying a good weep. An hour later, it's back to normal and life goes on in the same old way.

Whether for us the ice has broken or the light has dawned, let our ideals be of the authentic kind. The end of every service we attend ought to stir us to ask Paul's question on the road to Damascus: 'What shall I *do*, Lord?'

27

What is an elephant like?

I might have known that someone would write in. I had been presenting a radio series on laughter, and I happened to say that the story of Jonah had its funny moments. Listen to the prophet as he prays with a necessarily muffled voice from deep inside the whale.

Poor Jonah was heaved overboard from the ship taking him to Tarshish, the back of beyond, trying to escape from God, as if God were territorially imprisoned; or as if his home address lay in Israel and he was confined there like a human being with no means of transport. God had commissioned the prophet to go to Nineveh and denounce the wicked city, but Jonah would have no truck with preaching to any other than his own, the divinely chosen people. So he was on the run.

The crew dumped our unfortunate prophet in the sea, sadly not viciously, because they believed that the storm they had run into was his god's doing. They lived in a world of many gods. To appease his god the travelling Jonah must be sacrificed.

But it wasn't that I found humour in the prophet's plight. Letters of protest were written to the BBC because I had described the Book of Jonah as a fictional short story. I had firmly placed it in the category of a Chaucerian Canterbury tale rather than of something like the Battle of Hastings. One of my Bible commentaries warns us against 'applying the yardstick of zoological science to a tale which is neither scientific nor even historical but a parable like the Good Samaritan or the Prodigal Son'.

A man from Jarrow marched protestingly against me in print accusing me of contradicting Jesus who happened to refer to the Jonah story, as if that made it factual and not fiction. Jesus told stories in typically Jewish fashion to convey the truth to us. Do we dismiss the parables because they are not 'true' in the sense of reports of events that literally took place?

The account of the Prodigal Son may well be a story, though it tells of the kind of thing that happens all the while, not just once upon a time. My correspondent from Jarrow attached to his letter a press cutting which told of a whaler off the Falklands in February 1891 who was actually swallowed by a whale. The unfortunate creature was harpooned and cut up only to yield up the hapless whaler, still alive but deeply unconscious. They doused him with cold water and he came round. But what does that prove? It doesn't even prove that a human being can survive inside a whale for three days, for this was a matter of a few hours; and it certainly doesn't show that such a man can offer a prayer from inside it while he is there.

Jonah's whale is more accurately a 'big fish' and Jonah, so the tale goes, spent a miserable weekend inside it. The whale, or whatever it was, has always been the red herring in this story. Fillet it out, and you lose nothing of value. George Caird, who was one of our leading theologians at Oxford, once commented that readers of the Book of Jonah have been too preoccupied with problems of marine biology to get the real point of the story. Jonah was a bigotted nationalist, he wrote, who had to learn the hard lesson that God's loving purpose applied to all humankind, and not exclusively to any Chosen People,

Let us rapidly change the scene to the headquarters of the Roman governor Pontius Pilate. Among the many questions he asked Jesus, held in custody, was the leading one about truth. Jesus had said: ' My task is to bear witness to the truth. For this I was born; for this I came into the world, and all who are not deaf to truth listen to my voice.' Pilate, in reply, asked the big question: 'What is truth?' (John 18: 37-8) Was Pilate, whom Francis Bacon called Jesting Pilate, being cynical, as if to say, 'Who cares about truth anyway?' a question which hovers uncomfortably over today's cheap tabloids ?

My indignant correspondents, rushing to their computers or ball-point pens, appeared not to appreciate the profundity of that question any more maybe than the Roman governor did. A Glaswegian accused me of labelling the Jonah story as 'fictitious', which I never did and never would. There is a marked difference between 'fictional' and 'fictitious'. The first means a story which is nevertheless true in the deeper sense. The latter means something which is false in every sense. My Scottish critic expressed it simply if not naively by saying: 'Surely, by believing in the Bible we are being absolutely faithful to God, but on the other hand if we disbelieve part of the Bible, we are being unfaithful to God.' A lady from leafy Bucks accused me of 'believing bits of the Bible to be not quite true'.

The problem for my correspondents seemed to be a failure to grasp that the truth is a multilayered, many-splendoured thing; that, in fact, fact itself isn't the only kind of truth. Oscar Wilde is on record as saying that 'the English are always degrading the truth into facts'.

It is high time we came to a classic Hindu tale. We come ashore from that big fish to a big animal on land.

In an Indian village lived five blind men. One day they came upon a creature which somebody informed them was an elephant. 'What is an elephant like?' they asked. They were invited to feel its body. The first blind man said, 'Why, an elephant is like a pillar.' He had got hold of its leg. 'No, no, it's like a barrel,' another one said, having felt only its huge girth. The third man, gripping the elephant's tail, said, 'It's like a rope.' The fourth chipped in, 'It's like a hose,' for he had felt its trunk. And the fifth man cried out, 'It's like a winnowing fan.' He had felt only the ear. All five began to argue among themselves. Each insisted that his description of the elephant was the true one. It is the same with the Truth, capital T, says the Hindu. His ancient books, the Vedas, state that 'The Truth is One; people call it by various names.' The trouble is that, like those blind men, we find part of the truth and are apt to think we have grasped it all.

What is the truth about Jesus? This is a question of the heaviest import. He himself is recorded as asking the Pharisees: 'What do you think of the Messiah?' (Several contemporary translations use the word 'opinion' here, but this, it seems to me, belittles the question.) Jesus himself didn't respond to Pilate's question about the nature of truth. He had already answered it in the Upper

Room in that plain unequivocal statement 'I am the truth', amazing for any man to make, assuming that he did so, just like that! For any man, that is, who is either a psychopath suffering from megalomania or else the actual embodiment of the ultimate truth. As it has often been stressed, there is no neat halfway compromise between these two extremes. Jesus Christ is either one or the other. Orthodox Christianity, tried and tested over the centuries, declares with rocklike confidence that he is the other. The Other with an upper-case O. In brief, he is God.

There are affirmations ancient and modern, to this effect. Ambrose, Bishop of Milan, wrote: 'As the print of the seal on the wax is the express image of the seal itself, so Christ is the express image – the perfect representation of God.' Such a conviction is simply a sample of so many like it from the early centuries. Those who thought hard and long about Jesus Christ, and who in their own innermost souls had experienced the love and power of his presence, were unable to account for him in terms any the less. The seventeenth-century writer Blaise Pascal felt compelled to declare that 'Jesus Christ is the centre of all, and the goal to which all tends'. Oxford divinity professor Maurice Wiles echoes the same thought today when he says that Christ is the 'centre of God's presence and action in the world'.

Jesus of Nazareth has been the centre, sometimes the storm-centre, of endless argument, discussion and dispute about who he was, who he is, how he stands in relation to the truth about all things. Even those uneasy about making the shorthand statement that Christ is God have been driven to make major, unique claims for him. The distinguished Quaker Kenneth Barnes saw Jesus as a kind of super-Shakespeare, a person of great genius gifted with tremendous insight into human nature, conveying his message about the world while at the same time being totally involved in it.

We are in the end driven back to doubting Thomas's mighty profession of faith in the Upper Room when, confronted by the nail-prints, he cried out, 'My Lord and my God!'

28
The fainting house

One sunny spring morning we drove over to the village of Shimpling, just a mile or two away. We went to see the Fainting House. I had read about this small brick building in one of John Timpson's travel books pinpointing the unusual, the unlikely and the undeniably odd among the buildings and places up and down our land. This Fainting House so-called can be seen across the churchyard of St George's at Shimpling. (The Suffolk Shimpling, not the other one in Norfolk.)

Built in the 1840s, it contains a fireplace, seating, a cloakroom and an earth closet. Its original use may have been as a Sunday schoolroom; or possibly for local rectors to rest in, as one service ended and another was due a little later. But the author of this book *Timpson's Other England* explains why it is so named.

It seems that languishing Victorian ladies, excessively uptight in the suffocating clothes of the period, were apt to feel faint on hot summer Sundays during overlong services. 'They were sometimes overcome,' writes Mr Timpson, 'by the lack of air in the church – and (he adds cheekily) possibly by the surfeit of hot air coming from the pulpit.' So, he says, 'they were assisted across the churchyard into the Fainting House to recover.'

While there on that sunny spring morning, it occurred to me that the Bible has much to say about fainting and the factors in life that weaken us as we make our way on its lengthy, winding journey.

Factor One: *hunger* weakens.

In Mark's Gospel, we read of Jesus feeding four thousand as well as five. We needn't pause to speculate whether there were two such feedings of large crowds or whether the two are one and the same. Rather let us listen to what Jesus said to his men: 'I feel sorry for these people, because they have been with me for three days and now have nothing to eat. If I send them home without feeding them, they will faint as they go, because some of them have come a long way.'

Napoleon was faced with a similar problem. He expected his soldiers to move fast. They had to endure forced marches which entailed living in the countryside where supplies soon ran out. Because they lacked nourishment, his men fell ill. 'An army marches on its stomach,' he famously declared, and he proceeded to offer a prize of 20,000 francs to anyone who could come up with some inventive means of preserving food. A chef in Paris won the money, He worked out a plan for bottling food which had been previously heated. It was in London later that the plan was further refined by substituting tins for bottles, and from this came the canning industry.

Physical hunger isn't the only kind. To us who live in the rich countries, Mother Teresa once bluntly announced: 'Your poverty is greater than ours ... the spiritual poverty of the West is much greater than the physical poverty of the East. In the West, there are millions of people who suffer loneliness and emptiness, who feel unloved and unwanted. They are not hungry in the physical sense; what is missing is a relationship with God and each other,'

In Gethsemane Jesus said to three of his battered and bewildered disciples: 'The spirit is willing, but the flesh is weak.' Have we not perhaps turned that saying around? The flesh in our society is only too willing: it is spiritual weakness that we suffer from. How we need what Jesus meant when he spoke of the Bread of life.

Factor Two: *weariness* weakens. To the Galatians, Paul pleaded: 'Let us not become tired of doing good.' Or, as the old Bible has it, 'Let us not be weary in well doing; for in due season we shall reap, if we faint not' (Galatians 6: 9). The writer, one feels certain, didn't just mean the natural tiredness of spent physical energies, the weariness of a body in need of rest and sleep. There is a fatigue of the spirit, brought on perhaps by sheer boredom with the enterprise in hand.

And that brings me to William Maxwell Aitken better known as Lord Beaverbrook, the newspaper magnate and politician who set out to make a fortune when he was fifty and who suggested that any man who failed to do so could be written off as indeed a failure. He died in his mid-eighties in 1964.

A biography simply titled *Beaverbrook* eight years later tells us much about this notable if appalling Canadian whiz-kid. Its author was A J P Taylor who wrote that his subject never stuck at anything for very long. In politics he never fought a controversy through to a finish. He was constantly announcing that he was giving up control of his newspapers. At the dinner table he often lost interest in the middle of a conversation and fell asleep, or appeared to do so. 'He understood himself,' wrote his biographer, quoting his subject as having said, 'I am always excited at the beginning of a journey and bored after the first few miles.'

Lesser mortals than Lord Beaverbrook could make a similar confession. It takes some doing, does it not (be honest now) to be persistently faithful at any task. Sheer boredom sets in, and we are inclined to give up too readily. This is all too true in the living of the Christian life with its disciplines of devotion, churchgoing and altruistic service.

It has ever been so, right from the start. That other notable man, Paul the pioneer missionary, knew the danger of giving into weariness of spirit by giving up. 'Stand firm and steady,' he wrote to his beloved but troublesome Corinthians. 'Keep busy always in your work for the Lord, since you know that nothing you do in the Lord's service is ever useless.' (1 Corinthians 15: 58)

There came a critical period in American history. A renowned preacher stood up to address the students of Yale. 'The pillars of the State are shaken,' he declared. 'What can a good man do?' Then, leaning over the pulpit, he answered his own question quietly, 'He can go on being good.'

Which brings me to a final factor liable to make us falter and faint in the way.

Factor Three: *discouragement* weakens. Whoever wrote the Letter to the Hebrews (was it a woman?) must have been well aware of this. It is addressed to those who stand in danger of abandoning their Christian faith, so it speaks to our time. The author exhorts us to keep our eyes fixed on Jesus who did not give up despite even the horror of a cross.   'So do not let yourself become discouraged,' he (or possibly she) says, 'and give up.' The phrase in the old Bible is 'lest ye be wearied and faint.' (Hebrews 12: 3)

With great gusto we sing John Bunyan's hymn of pilgrimage, a favourite of Winston Churchill's and many another. But let us pause and take more careful note than often we do of what Bunyan is actually saying in his hymn, originally a poem in *The Pilgrim's Progress*. Come wind, come weather, the true Christian pilgrim will not be put off.   No lion or giant, neither hobgoblin nor foul fiend, no dismal stories or threats can halt him on his journey from earth to heaven.

These brave sentiments tie in with Bunyan's own response to the opposition that set in against him with the Restoration of the Monarchy in 1660. When a warrant was issued against him in November of that year for his unlawful preaching, he stubbornly refused to desist and was put in Bedford gaol for three months. Under threat of exile, and even of execution by hanging, he still would not be silenced. As he left the court on his way to the cell, where he was finally held for twelve years, he turned to the judge and said: 'I am at a point with you, for if I were out of prison today, I would preach the gospel again tomorrow.'

> *There's no discouragement*
> *shall make him once relent*
> *his first avowed intent*
> *to be a pilgrim.*

29
No small print

Across the years I find I have preached in several cathedrals and in a few Oxbridge college chapels. I have preached early on Easter Day at the Garden Tomb in Jerusalem to an international congregation, when a group of Americans from the southern Bible belt tried to hijack the service. I have preached to a congregation in Hungary through an interpreter, and over the airwaves in the United States. I have preached to a convention of master painters and house decorators in Yorkshire, and to a conference of Judges and magistrates in Cambridge. To come to the point (and to the end of this unseemly immodesty), if ever I am asked to preach to a company of insurance executives, (a most unlikely request, I grant you), I have already decided how to begin, what my opening sentence will be.

In the charter for living he left us as his bequest, I shall say, Jesus didn't include any small print. On your contract, or at the foot of your insurance policy, or in any number of legal documents, there are by necessity lengthy explanations, expositions, exceptions and exemptions. I say 'by necessity' sympathetically to those who must devise and draw up these documents. Life is complicated; and the ingenuity of the human mind is more than capable of getting round the law, evading payment, justifying non-payment. Detailed interpretations of general principles therefore become necessary.

The lawyer who approached Jesus to try to catch him out was trading in small print. What must he do to receive eternal life? Well, replied Jesus, what do the Scriptures say? Yes, that's right – love God, love your neighbour. But the enquirer wanted to justify himself, so he asked a supplementary question: 'Who is my neighbour?' Being a legal eagle, he had run his finger down to the exemption clauses. Like that eccentric Hollywood actor of yesterday, W C Fields, who on his deathbed was seen to be reading a Bible. It surprised those who were looking on, and he was asked why. He replied, 'I'm looking for a loophole.' Sinners that we are, aren't we all? Bob Hope once wisecracked: 'I do benefits for all religions – I'd hate to blow the hereafter on a technicality.'

What that lawyer was looking for was the answer to a totally opposite question. He was really asking Jesus, 'Who is not my neighbour?' Like the slogan which once appeared beside the Wailing Wall in Jerusalem and which read: 'Love thy fellow-Jew as thyself'. Exemption clauses again, and they are designed to protect self-interest, not to love and serve neighbours.

There is no one in the world who is not my neighbour. Jesus demanded that we love even our enemies. Thus he taught, with direct and uncompromising commands. From first to last he was radical in his teaching. Carry it, give it, lend it. Don't judge others. Ask, seek, knock. Sell all, follow me. He was following the early Jewish tradition which was full of direct and simple moral instructions. The book of Leviticus is full of them. They are regulations for the priests in the correct procedures to follow in dealing with sacrifices, offerings and ritual uncleanness.

We pause to observe that many of these instructions are not for us. We don't need to be told not to cut the hair on the sides of our heads or to trim our beards or tattoo ourselves or cut gashes on our bodies, all as part of the ritual of mourning. And there are regulations about ritual cleansing and sacrifice which deserve complete neglect. Nevertheless, the commandments about stealing, cheating, lying still apply and always will, for the good and peaceful order of any society. Furthermore, it is in Leviticus that we find the first mention of the second most important commandment of all: 'thou shalt love thy neighbour as thyself' (19: 18)

The odd thing about Leviticus is its mixture of wise and permanently important commandments interleaved with the almost comically absurd ritual requirements. William Neil, in his One *Volume Bible Commentary*, wrote that when it came to be regarded as equally vital to wear the right kind of garment of unmixed materials as to love one's neighbour, the Law is no longer divine revelation but human nonsense.

Colin Morris, in one of his brilliant Thoughts for the Day, said of the Law: 'You can even suffer a death sentence for not wearing the correct trousers in the temple – if you think I'm inventing that, read Exodus 28: 42.'

Man invariably complicates simple things. This is what happened with the lawmakers of ancient Israel. They introduced oceans of small print. One of their simple rules was: no work on the Sabbath. But then they had to define what work was, and they did so in a thousand clauses, and in the most ridiculous way. When Jesus came, he cut through those clauses and declared that the Sabbath was made for man, not man for the Sabbath. Even today, some Christians haven't caught up with him on that issue.

Much misery has been caused by restrictive attitudes to Sunday, which anyway isn't the Sabbath.

I read the other evening about the Presbyterian minister in Hawick in the Border country. He was no mean cellist, and he was practising one Sunday afternoon when a knock came on the manse door. Outside stood a group of his elders dressed in black and looking like a sort of Caledonian Mafia. They wore stern expressions on long faces. 'Ye'll not be playing your instrument on the Lord's Day, minister,' they said, menacingly before leaving. Pale and shaken, he hurriedly packed his cello in its case. Those wretched elders appeared to have forgotten that Calvin and Knox and their fellow-fathers of Presbyterianism, used to play bowls in Geneva on a Sunday evening.

But to return to my proposed sermon to the insurers, and its opening sentence. In the charter for living he left us as his bequest, Jesus didn't include any small print. Whatever I try to say in the rest of the sermon, I shall stress that the gospel is primarily about regeneration of soul not reformation of character. What must come first is our response to the love of God, not our resolution, as at the new year, to do better, strive after excellence, struggle to attain the perfection expected of us. We need to be 'born again'. Yes, I am afraid so. I know that the 'born again Christian' isn't always an attractive creature and can be singularly off-putting. But we need that spiritual rebirth which means an entry into a new and loving relationship with God in Christ.

Perhaps I might end that hypothetical sermon by telling my insurance executives about T Z Koo, an outstanding Chinese Christian leader of the twentieth century. I read of him in one of Leonard Griffith's volumes of sermons.

Koo described what won him to Christianity during his years as a student. The Christian religion made him an offer different from any put to him by other faiths. Confucianism, the creed on which he had been brought up, was concerned only with moral rights and wrongs – the small print. But Dr Koo testified that he had no peace or joy by straining or striving to be good. In fact, he felt wretched and miserable every time he failed, which was often. Then along came a missionary one day who told him that, if only he would open his heart to a Personality, the morals would come right. Koo responded and accepted Jesus Christ, The problem of morality then ceased to torment him. He had entered into a new relationship with God, and was able to tackle the charter for living given by Christ with hope and joy.

Somebody once remarked: 'Man is an able creature, but he has made 32,647,389 laws and hasn't yet improved on the Ten Commandments.' Or, we should add, on the Sermon on the Mount, with no small print and with standards which, though not readily attainable, aren't totally unattainable by anyone, God being helper.

30
The valley of decision

'Multitudes, multitudes in the valley of decision.' Those words, in Joel 3: 14 in the Authorized Version, have long intrigued me. It is a vivid picture. A huge crowd caught in a valley where some kind of decision faces them. Some translations use the word 'judgement' rather than 'decision'.

This valley is up our street. It refers to the last great battle of mankind where, so they believed, God will pronounce his final judgement upon humanity. We are referring here to Armageddon, located at Megiddo in the Palestinian plain of Esdraelon, where they say the forces of good and evil will fight it out to the end. We are assured that good will win and the Kingdom of God will be established. Megiddo in ancient times was the scene of many battles of decisive importance.

Whatever the prophet's meaning may have been in terms of that final divine judgement, every day expects decisions from us, mainly small but sometimes far from so.

I think back now to the junior days in the late fifties of our two older sons. Philip the younger always knew at once what he wanted in the local sweet shop. His elder brother Martin, however, took a while, quite a while sometimes, to make his choice at the counter. We'd take them into Anne's, a rather superior confectioner's on The Grove in Ilkley. Philip would instantly snap up his purchase; but Martin would stand at the counter for what seemed an age, a queue building up behind him of which he was heedless. There he was, in the valley of decision with the multitude, unable to decide between a Lucky Bag and a stick of Spanish. We all face such problems as we shop downtown. I read the other day in a book of reflections on everyday life that 'one of life's difficult decisions is picking the superstore check-out line that will move fastest'. Haven't we all been faced with that one, every Friday and at other times?

Life, I need scarcely say, is more than a shop queue. It demands major decisions from us from time to time. Paul, early in his Letter to the Philippians, had his own decision to make. Would it be better for him to die and be completely with Christ, or should he stay in this world to minister to them? 'I am pulled in two directions,' he informs us, using an expressive metaphor. The Greek text contains a picture of a traveller in a narrow, rocky defile with walls of rock on either side, hedging him tightly in, so that he can only go on or go back.

You and I are faced, at crucial stages of our life's journey, with significant, far-reaching decisions. At school quite early on in these days, choices must be made about the chief subjects to be studied, as these can profoundly affect a youngster's whole future. Later on, young people choose their marriage partners and, as the divorce rate shows, too many mistakes are made. In some cultures in our multicultural society, marriage partners are chosen by parents. Then there are career decisions, whether to take this appointment or that, to stay put or to move.

Looking down upon this spinning globe from a great height, do we not see the multitudes in their valley of many decisions daily, great and small, and some agonizing, and some fateful? The words of James Russell Lowell must give us profound pause.

> Once to every man and nation comes the moment to decide.
> In the strife of Truth with Falsehood, for the good or evil side.

Decisions have by necessity to be settled, but *to remain undecided is a decision in itself.*

The Fosdick family lived at Buffalo in New York State, and young Harry grew up to be a number one preacher in the USA. In one of many books he wrote, he put it this way: 'A man who, rowing down Niagara River, debates within himself whether or not he will stop at Buffalo, and who cannot decide, thereby has decided. His irresolution has not for a moment interfered with the steady flow of the river, and if he debates long enough concerning his stop at Buffalo, he will awake to discover that the decision not to stop there has been taken from him. Fosdick might have added that, in this particular location, the steady flow of the river would soon take the indecisive man over the Niagara Falls to his watery doom.

In other words, not to decide is nonetheless to do so. Olin Miller remarked that 'when a person tells you, "I'll think it over and let you know" – you know.' I daresay we've all been on both the giving and receiving ends here. I must confess that I have said that very thing more than once. I might as well have avoided that procrastinating reply and said no straightaway.

In the making of difficult decisions, *we need to pray*. When he was dramatically confronted by his Lord on the Damascus road, Paul asked, 'What shall I do, Lord?'

When they were drawing up the Constitution of the United States, the Convention called together to formulate it reached crisis point in June 1787. Representatives of the thirteen original States had been haggling for a month, but to no avail. It was on the morning of 16th June that Benjamin Franklin made a key speech addressed to George Washington. 'Mr President' he said, 'the small progress we have made after four or five weeks' close attention and continual reasoning with each other is, methinks, a melancholy proof of the imperfections of human undertaking. In this situation ... as it were in the dark to find political truth ... how has it happened, sir, that we have not hitherto thought of humbly applying to the Father of Light to illuminate our understanding.' In consequence, prayers were instituted at the start of every day's business in that pioneering assembly. In the making of decisions, we can do with much prayer. It steadies us, clears our fogged mental apparatus, conditions us to a calm approach to the problem and makes a wise and right decision more likely.

There is, last but not least the question of *deciding for Christ and his Church*.

Evangelists demand decisions for Christ from their mass congregations. We may feel sometimes that preachers like Billy Graham have tended to push their hearers too hard, insisting on urgency and warning that it may be the only chance they will ever get to be saved. Does the good Lord, who works quietly and patiently upon us in other ways, twist our arms and hustle us to say yes to him. This is open to discussion, if only because we are such devilish procrastinators.

Nevertheless, the demand for decisions for or against God may often be found in the Bible, and there is pressure and urgency about it too.

On Mount Carmel, the prophet Elijah cried out: 'How much longer will it take you to make up your minds? If the Lord is God, worship him; but if Baal is God, worship him!' (I Kings 18: 21)

Earlier, with the invasion of the Promised Land accomplished, Joshua says to the people: 'Decide today whom you will serve.' And as if to bias their choice, he adds, 'As for my family and me, we will serve the Lord.' (Joshua 24: 15)

Turning the pages still farther back, we come upon Moses putting an ultimatum to the people. 'I am now giving you the choice between life and death,' he tells them, '... and I call heaven and earth to witness the choice you make.' He then gives them no choice at all. 'Choose life,' he concludes tersely (Deuteronomy 30: 19). It's slightly like the notorious line in Mario Puzo's novel *The Godfather* in which the latter says, 'I'll make him an offer he can't refuse.' Or rather like a former and formidable Prime Minister in a TV programme filmed at home at Number Ten purporting to show the Thatchers in the intimacy of their domestic life. 'Where shall we go for holidays this year, dear?' she asks. Before Denis can take a breath, she says, 'We'll go to Cornwall,' On cue he replies, 'Yes, dear.'

Decisions, decisions, a valley of judgement full of them. But God never twists our arm. Lord Gorell said: 'God is no Master of puppets, nor need we dance to his tune.' Our choice for or against him is free, no strings attached. C S Lewis, testifying to his own famous conversion from atheism to Christ, wrote: 'I was offered what now appears a moment of wholly free choice ... I could open the door or keep it shut ... no threat or promise was attached to either, though I knew that to open the door meant the incalculable.'

31

Where is God?

The ancient creeds baldly state that 'he ascended into heaven'. What does this really mean? How are we to interpret it? Did the physical body of Jesus, with its crucifixion blemishes still to be seen on hands and side, rise up and begin a long journey to the stars? At what speed would he have gone upwards? How many miles per hour, minutes or seconds? Would the disciples, standing there looking up at the sky, have kept him in view a lot longer if they'd had powerful binoculars? Where was the body heading? Heaven? Where's that? How far out, in and beyond the Milky Way, would it have needed to travel to reach its celestial destination? Is he there yet, or still journeying? How many light years in all this, whatever that means?

Questions, questions. A torrent of them surround what we celebrate at Ascensiontide. All of them spring from the credal statement: He ascended into heaven. We in the United Reformed Church omit any such explicit declaration in our Statement of Faith, nor is Ascension Day mentioned in our URC diaries. All these questions are reasonable and justified when we are faced with those four words: 'He ascended into heaven'. Mediaeval theologians seriously debated whether the ascending body of Jesus was clothed or naked. Brrr ... !

We have to interpret the imagery. The Ascension, whatever it was and whatever happened, signifies the truth that the *localised physical presence* of the Lord was now replaced by his *universal spiritual presence*. One Bible scholar wrote of the risen Christ going 'out of the here into the everywhere, out of some people's sight that he might be near to all people's hearts'. Or, as the great Archbishop William Temple explained: 'The ascension of Christ is his liberation from all restrictions of time and space. It does not represent his removal from the earth, but his constant presence everywhere on earth.'

All of this begs the broader question: where is God? Far above in highest heaven, beyond the bright blue sky? The whole idea of God is rejected by some entirely on this basis. We all recollect how the Russians in their space programme announced that they had found no trace of God in outer space. Their astronauts went looking for God as if God were some sort of a Being occupying space, as we beings do on earth. In a sense, to ask God where God is, is to ask an absurd question.

In primitive times, God was a local deity walking in the cool of the Garden of Eden with Adam and Eve hiding from him among the trees. Then we find him living amid thunder and lightning on top of Mount Sinai the firework display deity dear to Cecil B De Mille the movie mogul. And then we learn that he is a territorially confined God. As Israel's private possession, his power and efficacy must be restricted to Israel's borders, like a radio signal which cannot be picked up in Egypt, Assyria or Babylon. The tear-stained exiles virtually cried out: 'How can we sing a song to the Lord in a foreign land *when we are out of range of him and he can't hear us'?'*

Next, in the first line of Psalm 90, we stumble upon an amazing discovery in the search for God. The Psalmist prays: 'O Lord, you have always been our home.' So, after all, God was no longer at home or not at home, as if somewhere with a fixed abode, an address as it were. He was Home itself. Man stopped looking for him in some locality, realizing that he was so great that the entire creation was somehow contained within him, not he within his creation.

The Apostle Paul was later to share this insight with the learned thinkers of Athens. He said to them: 'God, who made the world and everything in it, is Lord of heaven and earth and does not live in man-made temples.' Then he added that God was actually not far from any one of them, and he quoted some non-Christian source which said of God that 'in him we live and move and exist' (Acts 17: 24,28).

No wonder the disciples on the Mount of Olives were challenged with that question: 'Why are you standing there looking up at the sky? (Acts 1: 10-11) No one can expect to find God that way. Granted that signs of divine handiwork in all its staggering splendour may well be visible to the enlightened eye of the person of faith, he or she knows that God cannot be spotted anywhere in the creation, for the creation itself is contained within its Maker and Sustainer. 'In him we live and move and exist.'

Furthermore, God isn't _a_ being. John V Taylor, former Bishop of Winchester and a man with artistic as well as theological insights, once confessed: 'Gradually I have come to realize what I didn't realize as a young man – that when I am talking about God I am not taking about _a_ anything. That is precisely the difference. He isn't _a_ being, isn't even the Supreme Being. He Is Being itself, from which all things derive their existence.'

So, together we 'explore' God, a better word to use than 'seek'. But this view of God as Being with a capital B is too much for our tiny minds to take in. It makes this concept of God seem far removed from us. In deepest need we need a God we can go to in prayer, with whom we commune and converse in intimate, spontaneous language.

In a volume of his sermons, Dr Leonard Griffith, one-time minister of the City Temple, tells a story about Abraham Lincoln. One day the President's little son Tad lost a fisticuff argument with another boy. He went at once to the Oval office. He said to Secretary Chase, 'I want my father.' A Yale lecturer telling the story asks us to imagine the kind of reply that simple request might have received. Chase could have said: 'My little fellow, I will tell the Chief Executive of the nation, who will soon prove himself to me, his servant, the master of unparalleled difficulties in finance, that you wish to see him.' Like any other little lad with a bloody nose, it is highly likely that he would have reiterated his cry, – 'I want my father.'

Again, suppose the defeated, dejected Tad had encountered Seward, the Secretary of State, and said, 'I want my father.' Seward could have replied: 'I will get for you the most remarkable diplomatic mind who ever warded off from a young nation in sore straits the attack of the British Empire.' Still the smitten, mud-stained boy would have cried, 'I want my father.' Then suppose that the plaintive appeal had reached the ears of Stanton, Lincoln's War Secretary. He might well have said, 'I will get for you the Commander-in-Chief of the Armies of the United States.' To Stanton, such was the President. Can you imagine the persistent plea, now a desperate sob? 'I want my father.'

The Lord God who made heaven and earth and all things is Creator, Sustainer, Provider. He is omnipotent, all-knowing, all-seeing, the Ground of our being, the great Original, Author and Finisher, Alpha and Omega, the Ultimate Reality. Numerous are his titles, many his attributes, and they undoubtedly contain the truth about God. Yet in time of need we find them all unhelpful save one. God is our Father, we his children; and even though we cannot define God, we can come to him in a loving relationship, as children may come to a loving father.

It was this that Jesus disclosed to us. And, we believe, it is this relationship that Jesus came to establish between God and humankind. To a puzzled Philip who said to him, 'Lord show us the Father, that is all we need', he replied, 'Whoever has seen me has seen the Father' (John 14: 8-9).

So, where is God? In him it is true, we live and move and exist. In Christ he comes to us as Father. But he comes also with a commission, a task to tackle, an objective to achieve.

The Ascension doesn't mark an ending so much as a beginning. Assuredly, it represents the cessation of the appearances made by the risen Lord to his disciples (though not, we note, to Pilate, the Romans or the priests). The Ascension also points to the coming of enabling power at Pentecost, observed ten days after Ascension Day, to initiate and sustain the worldwide mission of the Church. For this they are bidden to wait patiently back in Jerusalem for the word 'go'.

'Go, then to all peoples everywhere and make them my disciples....;

32

Full of the Spirit

The sound of a hurricane, the sight of flames of fire, the babble of languages said to be spoken by people who didn't know them – what does this mean? More important, what does it mean to be 'filled with the Holy Spirit', and who is, and how can we tell?   The questions come hurtling towards us like the rushing mighty wind of Pentecost. These Whitsun questions congregate to be answered; or if that's beyond us, we can respond with replies. On that very day itself two thousand years ago, the eye and ear witnesses to the event were just as puzzled as we are today.

'All filled with the Holy Spirit.' Does this mean *they were put on an emotional high?*

J G Whittier was a nineteenth-century journalist and editor who wrote poems and hymns. Best known is 'Dear Lord and Father of mankind.' Behind it lies a story of surprises.

In the neighbourhood where he lived in Massachusetts, some noisy and hysterical revivalist meetings had been held. Whittier was disturbed by them. He was a Quaker more inclined to a rational approach to religious faith, favouring silent and reflective worship. Consequently, he was prompted to write a poem of comment called *The Brewing of Soma* about these phenomena. Soma was an intoxicating African drink, supposed to excite heady religious feeling. It was imbibed also by American Indians to enable them, as they believed, to have union with the Deity. In one verse of his poem, Whittier wrote,

> *In sensual transports wild as vain*
> *We brew in many a Christian fane,*
> *The heathen Soma still.*

Then follows the familiar verse,

Dear Lord and Father of mankind,
Forgive our foolish ways.

When we realize what has gone before in the poem, we appreciate the significance of the author's references to 'the silence of eternity', and the blessing falling 'noiseless', and 'ordered lives' confessing 'the beauty of God's peace'.

Was that day of Pentecost the first revivalist meeting? The disciples, ecstatic and babbling away in tongues (which is more likely than that they were suddenly multi-lingual), gave the impression that they were drunk. The accusation was indignantly rebuffed. But is this what it means to be full of the Spirit? If so, many quieter Christians will be left out in the cold.

Emotional 'highs' at religious meetings may be basically no different from pop concert hysteria, demon spirit possession and the behaviour of people under hypnosis and drugs. Such was the view taken by a world authority on the psychology of possession, Dr William Sargant, who wrote that 'reason is dethroned, the normal brain computer is temporarily put out of action, and new ideas are uncritically accepted.' This can hardly be what happened on that day of Pentecost in Jerusalem.

'All filled with the Holy Spirit.' Does this mean *they were given a superior knowledge of God?*

No human being can ever claim this. God is infinitely greater than we can conceive, and our finite and limited minds cannot encompass him. We may know him certainly, for he continually discloses himself to us in many ways, and this is the unceasing operation of the Holy Spirit. But we shall never capture God in our own private little box, and so claim to possess a superior knowledge of him. The mystics and the most deeply spiritual people, and those who live daily near to God, never do. In the divine presence, they resemble President Roosevelt and his scientist friend William Beebe.

After dinner they would go outside and share in a regular little ritual. They would gaze into the night sky, possibly with binoculars, and pinpoint a faint spot of light-mist below the lower left-hand corner of the great square of Pegasus. Then one of them would recite: 'That is the Spiral Galaxy of Andromeda. It is as large as our Milky Way. It is one of a hundred million galaxies. It is seven hundred and fifty thousand light years away. It consists of one hundred billion suns each larger than our sun.' Having done the recital, they would pause in silence; then Roosevelt would grin and say: 'Now I think we are small enough, let's go inside!'

The function of the Holy Spirit isn't to disclose to us a superior knowledge of God but to *lead us into all the truth*. It is a gradual, unfolding process. The truth isn't static but dynamic. We cannot be given it in one dollop, so to speak, once and for all. We can only receive a little at a time. We need 'topping up'. 'I have much more to tell you,' said Jesus, 'but now it would be too much for you to bear.'

Dr E V Rieu was the editor and translator of many best-selling classics in paperback. He died in 1972, and *The Times* obituary said: 'An agnostic for half his life, he became an Anglican at the age of sixty, made a new translation of the *The Four Gospels*, and was a member of the joint Churches Committee for the new translation of the Bible.' One of Rieu's sons heard that his father was going to undertake, single-handed, a translation of the Gospels, and he said: 'It will be very interesting to see what father makes of the Gospels. It will be still more interesting to see what the Gospels make of father.'

Well, the Holy Spirit used scripture, as he so often does, to unfold the truth gradually to the agnostic scholar as he worked on the project, finally transforming him into a fully committed Christian. That's how the Holy Spirit works, progressively revealing God, but not giving any of us a superior knowledge of him in an instant.

'All filled with the Holy Spirit.' Does this mean that *only Christians possess the truth?*

At a meeting in Cheltenham I couldn't help overhearing a conversation between two women, both actively Church of England. One was talking about an engagement, or was it a marriage? The young woman was marrying a young man from the Middle East, I gathered; and he was said to be 'a very nice boy'. The only snag was, it seemed, that he was a practising Muslim. One of these two talking about it mentioned this fact with as much concern as if the boy had a criminal record or was infected with AIDS. It was assumed without question that Christianity was the one and only right way to the true God and Islam was terribly wrong. I thought to myself, at least the girl was marrying a young fellow with a faith he takes seriously and not some secularized materialist yuppie of the West who may be totally ignorant of his Christian heritage, and may even scorn it.

But *isn't* Jesus Christ the only true way to God? He is the Way, the Truth and the Life, and no one comes to the Father except by him. Granted. I hope I shall never adopt or fall into an arrogantly superior attitude to other religions. I see their followers sometimes putting us to shame by manifesting in their daily lives the Christian spirit more positively than I do. Jesus said, and he repeated it for emphasis, 'You will recognize them by their fruit.' Followers of other faiths may demonstrate better than we do the fruits of the Spirit as listed by the Apostle Paul – love, joy, peace, patience, kindness, goodness, faithfulness, humility and self-control. These are sure signs of those filled with the Holy Spirit, and they will not necessarily be Christians.

Harry Williams, the priestly Cambridge theologian who became a monk, wrote about what he termed the 'Christ Reality' which he found, he said, in the Old Testament prophets, in the Buddha and Lao-Tse and Mohammed and many others outside Christianity. Nor is the Christ-Reality absent, he affirmed, from the discoveries and insights of a Charles Darwin, or a Karl Marx, or a Sigmund Freud, still less from the music of a Mozart or a Beethoven or the plays of a Shakespeare or even a Bernard Shaw. Not that all these were always right, nor was everything they said true. But the Christ-Reality was there, intermingled with the faulty judgements and the grievous errors.

They were all filled with God the Holy Spirit, who cannot be captured and confined, like a butterfly in a churchy Christian box. For this, we give thanks at Whitsun, the church's birthday.

33

Coping with the climate

In his *Brief Encounter*, Noel Coward wrote: 'I believe we should all behave quite differently if we had lived in a warm, sunny climate all the time.' But, centuries earlier, was Jonathan Swift right when he ascribed the absence of worthy poetry to prolonged winter cold?

> *Say, Britain, could you ever boast-*
> *Three poets in an age at most?*
> *Our chilling climate hardly bears*
> *A sprig of bays in fifty years.*

Lord Byron in lighter vein offered his own cheeky comment on climate. He made adultery rhyme with sultry in his *Don Juan*, claiming that an oppressive atmosphere makes for increased sexual shenanigans.

Thus we come to Perga in Pamphylia, and to a spot of biblical detective work. In Acts 13 we can read an account of the apostle Paul's first try at peripatetic evangelism. With Barnabas and John Mark he travelled from Antioch (Syrian) to Antioch (Pisidian) by way of Cyprus. Leaving the port of Paphos at its western end, they sailed about 160 miles northwards to the southern coast of what is now the rugged land of Turkey. Their first stop was Perga a few miles inland; and the first question is why they didn't stop there to preach Christ and gather a company of recruits to the Christian cause. They moved on almost immediately, taking one of ancient Asia's toughest journeys, more than enough to daunt a first-century Michael Palin. They didn't, however, take John Mark any farther. He opted to return to Jerusalem, perhaps because he chickened out of the one hundred-mile trek over the Taurus mountains to the other Antioch. It stood on a plateau 3,600 feet above sea level.

The road, such as it was, attracted muggers and highwaymen in its wild and deserted state, much like that notorious way down from Jerusalem to Jericho. Even the redoubtable Alexander the Great had to fight his way along this Pamphylian route. There was also a difficult river to cross. In addition, we know that Paul was a sick man when he set out on that journey. In his Letter to the Galatians he wrote in the J B Phillips version: 'You know how handicapped I was by illness when I first preached the Gospel to you' (4: 12).

Was his sickness ophthalmia, or epilepsy? Or, most likely in the opinion of some scholars, malaria? Did this amazingly brave and determined man set out on that mountain journey with a malarial fever enough to make him weak and with a nasty headache? A traveller has described the headache as being like a red-hot bar thrust through the forehead, while someone else likened it to a dentist's drill boring through a man's temple.

But why did the ailing Paul leave the coastal plain and take that terrible journey, ill as he was? Sir William Ramsey, a famous classical archaeologist, sums it up in a single word – CLIMATE. Perga was a damp dump. It lay in low-lying country, marshy, humid and thoroughly unhealthy. The chances are that Paul, worn and weary after the mission in the difficult island of Cyprus, caught the disease in the muggy and oppressive atmosphere of Pamphylia. He had to get out and get up to a more bracing and cleaner climate.

Climate makes a lot of difference to a lot of things. Live in a poor climate and your health, your output, your bearing and your disposition are all affected. Live in a good one, and all these are benefitted. I can recall how different places in my own journey through life have affected me differently. I spent my early years in the heavy, enervating atmosphere of the Thames Valley. In the hot summer I felt regularly ill and tired. And that was when important school examinations were held. But when we went like Paul and Barnabas, northwards and upwards, into the Yorkshire Dales, what a difference!

I am sure that these differences affect the quality of church life. Let some clever sociologist do a survey of human temperament, health and output in relation to climate. I sense that in a bracing climate we church people are more lively and productive, and much easier to get on with. I think I might be able to prove the point from the history of my own pastoral relationships, but tact and the Protestant equivalent of the Catholic confessional forbid any such exercise.

Leaving such things to others better qualified to deal with them, I turn to Martin Luther King who had this to say about the mass media. 'Our minds are constantly being invaded by legions of half-truths, prejudices and false facts,' he observed. 'One of the great needs of mankind is to be lifted above the morass of false propaganda.' *Lifted above!* I borrow this imagery. Our need, you might say, is to be lifted above the putrid atmosphere of the plains of life in our contemporary society, and up and on to the plateau of a purer, cleaner climate.

An American magazine some time ago published an editorial entitled 'A Twisted Scale of Values'. I've kept the cutting, yellow with age, through the years. It mentioned a TV programme featuring Elvis Presley, then at the height of his fame as a sex-pop idol. In the course of an hour he sang two songs and waggled his hips a couple of times and was paid 125,000 dollars. I've nothing to say against Elvis himself. He attracted an enormous international audience of fans and still does, although he has been dead nearly thirty years. It was the amount of the payment which prompted the writer of that editorial to analyse it.

He claimed that it was equal to the annual salary of the President of the United States; three times the income of the Chief Justice; more than the wages of 25 rural schoolteachers; equivalent to the tuitions of 25 people at college; and enough to feed 3000 refugees for a whole year. In a sharp concluding sentence, the editorial said that 'this reveals the depth of decadence into which our Western scale of values has sunk'. It is arguably worse now. As I write, our morning newspaper has a front page headline about casinos. It refers to the 'terrifying dispatch from the US where organized crime, prostitution and misery pervade the casinos ... and where for every dollar gambling puts into the economy, three must be spent repairing the social havoc it wreaks'.

Depth and sunk! Lifted above! We are down on the unhealthy plain again, and we could do with that lift to the clearer air above.

There are fifteen Psalms in the Psalter that occupy a special category. They were composed to be sung on the march by pilgrims making their way to Jerusalem for the Passover, or for some such celebrated occasion. Hear them joyfully singing as they wend their way toward the glinting rooftops of the city, the dome of the Temple no doubt crowning the view and stirring their hearts.

'I was glad when they said to me, "Let us go to the house of the Lord!" Our feet are standing within your gates, O Jerusalem. Jerusalem – built as a city that is bound firmly together. To it the tribes go up ...'

Go up! That's it! The Holy City was built among hills. One imagines the upwardly mobile procession leaving the hot, stuffy and oppressive atmosphere of that hell-hole Jericho, below sea level and the unhealthiest spot for miles around, and climbing upwards into the better atmosphere of the high ground upon which Jerusalem stands.

These Psalms 120 to 134 are each headed 'A Song of Ascents'. They were 'going up songs' or 'uphill songs'. Geographically true, of course, but think beyond the physical fact to the symbolism here. We go up to worship, up to a healthier level. Worship is a lift. And such is the theme running through a hymn we've left behind in Congregational Praise 661. H M Butler wrote it for the *Harrow School Hymn Book (1881)* while he was Head Master there.

> *Above the level of the former years,*
> *The mire of sin, the slough of guilty fears,*
> *The mist of doubt, the blight of love's decay,*
> *O Lord of light, lift all our hearts today!*
>
> *Above the swamps of subterfuge and shame,*
> *The deeds, the thoughts, that honour may not name,*
> *The halting tongue that dares not tell the whole,*
> *O Lord of truth, lift every Christian soul.*

34

Everydayness

There is a fair deal of 'everydayness' in the Bible. In the book of Acts, for example, we read how *every day* they studied the scriptures to see if what Paul said was really true'.

That remarkable man from Tarsus on his missionary travels reached a nondescript place named Berea in northern Greece. Today, I believe, it's a quiet little agricultural town sitting on a mountain ledge. I understand that the people there show visitors a railed-off enclosure on a school playground where there are four massive steps. From these, they say, Paul preached. His name in Greek letters is faintly carved on the top step. The good folk of Berea, both Jews and Greeks, gave Paul and his partner in mission a friendly welcome. They were, it appears, keen students of the scriptures, meaning the Old Testament.

Some Christian people do read their Bibles daily, as they would their newspapers. There are daily notes available to help us understand what we read. I suspect, however, that many Christian people, even churchgoers, simply do not read the Bible but only hear it read by the minister or someone else in church. 'The Bible is like the poor,' commented Samuel Butler; 'we have it always with us, but we know very little about it'.

That, one fears, is only too true today, although those words were written well over a century ago. Thomas Carlyle, Butler's contemporary and fellow-author, noted in one of his Essays: 'In the poorest cottage are Books; is one Book wherein for several thousands of years the spirit of man has found light, and nourishment and an interpreting response to whatever is deepest in him.' The German philosopher Immanuel Kant pointed to the Bible as an inexhaustible fountain of all truths, its existence being humanity's greatest blessing.

There are always voices in our society writing the Bible off, even condemning it. In my pre-Suffolk days, I remember listening late at night to a phone-in programme on the Swindon radio station GWR which ought to stand for 'godless, witless rubbish', for that's what we used to get from its presenter. He made plastic pronouncements upon life in an immature and sometimes arrogant style. On one occasion, a caller mentioned the Bible, and he cracked back, 'You don't believe that stuff, do you?' He should visit the HQ of the Bible Society to have his ignorance replaced by knowledge. It is based in Swindon, and it has been celebrating its bicentenary.

I expect that Bible Society staff know about the couple who had their first offspring, a baby boy. His father was anti-religious and, discussing names, said to his wife: 'We'll not have any names from the Bible, like Matthew, Mark, Luke or John. We'll call him Stephen!'

The Bible is the book that tells us about God and man. In one of my books of quotations, William Lyon Phelps was quoted in the *New York Times* as saying: 'You can learn more about human nature by reading the Bible than by living in New York.'

The wise will note this and seek to read, mark, learn and inwardly digest the contents of this unique collection of divinely inspired writings – every day.

Christian discipleship, seriously undertaken, does make heavy demands upon us. 'If anyone wants to come with me,' said Jesus, 'he must forget self, take up his cross *every day*, and follow me.' Olwen Davies was thus self-forgetful.

She was a middle-aged district nurse who gets a deserved mention in A J Cronin's autobiography *Adventures in Two Worlds*. She had spent years on a tough job looking after the hard-pressed inhabitants of a Welsh mining village. Calm and cheerful, she toiled away with fortitude and patience, but she was badly paid, like many another vocational worker. Cronin himself was medical officer for the area, and he worried about her. He said to her, 'You ought to have an extra pound a week at least. God knows, you're worth it.' Smiling, but with an intense and grave expression in her gaze, she replied, 'Doctor, if God knows I'm worth it, that's all that matters to me.'

For most of us, ours is a Christianity of cushion rather than cross. A Jesuit priest, Anthony De Mello, records the lament of a bishop who gloomily remarked: 'Wherever Jesus went there was a revolution; wherever I go people serve tea!'

Jesus made heavy demands on his original disciples. When he talked of their need to take up a cross, it turned out literally true. Their allegiance to him resulted in martyrdom. For us it is highly unlikely to turn out like that, though Christian allegiance today does make its martyrs in some troubled places of the earth. The cross to be taken up daily is for us a metaphorical thing denoting possible pain and hardship.

Human nature resists all such. Naturally, we prefer cushions to crosses. There's a Jewish yarn about Goldstein aged 92 who had lived through pogroms in Poland, concentration camps in Germany and dozens of other persecutions against the Jews. 'Oh, Lord!' he said, 'isn't it true that we are your chosen people?' A heavenly voice replied: 'Yes, Goldstein, the Jews are my chosen people.' 'Well, then,' came the reply, 'isn't it time you chose somebody else?'

Another Jewish story tells us that when Moses threw his wand into the Red Sea the expected miracle did not take place. It was only when the first man threw himself into the sea that the waves receded and the water divided itself to offer a dry passage to the Jews.

Divine choice and allegiance to Christ for Christians means that demands, possibly rigorous, may well be made upon us. 'Man's highest life,' stated R H Benson, 'does not consist of self-expression, but in self-sacrifice.' We are bound to add – 'every day'.

The prophet waxed eloquent when his people drove a wedge between *worship* and *service*. In Isaiah chapter 58 it says: 'The Lord said, "They worship me *every day*, claiming that they are eager to know my ways and obey my laws." ' But then, the prophet says to them: 'At the same time ... you pursue your own interests and oppress your workers ... you quarrel and fight.'

The prophet's complaint was that, though the Lord's people crowded the places of worship and sacrifice, almost suffocating God with the smell of the right ritual sacrifices (almost a comic picture), their daily conduct and behaviour offended him. They treated the underdog unjustly, deprived orphans of their rights and oppressed widows. What the Lord wanted from them was the removal of the chains of oppression, the lifting of the yoke of injustice, the sharing of food with the hungry, practical compassion to the homeless and destitute. 'Then,' the Lord told them, 'my favour will shine on you like the morning sun ... When you pray, I will answer you. When you call to me, I will respond.'

A major lesson the people of the Old Testament had to learn was that just and loving conduct was more pleasing to God than any amount of formal worship. Hundreds of years went by, and they still hadn't learnt it even when Jesus was physically among them. His fierce criticism of the religious officials of the day was just this: 'They don't practise what they preach.' He quoted another bit of Isaiah to them. 'These people, says God, honour me with their words, but their heart is really far away from me' (29: 13).

Sunday worship in church, and weekday behaviour in our dealings with each other, belong tightly together and are not to be conveniently separated.

Geoffrey Bellhouse of Eastbourne, an outstanding Presbyterian among yesterday's preachers, had this passage in one of his sparkling sermons. 'There are still people who would not miss Communion, but who still refuse to stretch out a reconciling hand or write a reconciling letter. There are still people who "enjoy a good sermon" but who go home afterwards to bully the whole household.' The preacher pleaded with his congregation not to regard religion as a separate compartment of life, and that church services should never be viewed as ends in themselves. True religion, he concluded, 'seeks to baptise the whole of life into the spirit of Jesus'.

I am reminded of a tale about a devoutly religious woman who went to church every day. On her way children would call out to her, beggars would accost her; but she was so immersed in her devotions she failed to notice them. One morning she reached the church and pushed the door but it wouldn't open. She pushed it again harder, but she found the door locked. She was distressed at the thought of missing service for the first time in years. Then she looked up, and there it was. A note pinned to the door which simply said: 'I'm out there!'

35

Look to the mountains

In July 1938, a broadcast service was held thousands of feet up among the Swiss Alps, and the preacher said: 'The mountain psalm you have just heard sent its music down to the valleys from the most wonderful pulpit you could possibly imagine. We are here, high up on the Jungfraujoch, in a cathedral of snow-clad peaks, built by the Divine Creator's hand. No traffic of the streets, no noise of machinery can disturb the calm. The mountains stand around us, snow-clad and silent.'

There is a calming, refreshing aspect to hill and mountain. They bring the lyrical out of us. The Mountain Psalm is 121. We know it well in the Authorized Version. 'I will lift up mine eyes to the hills, from whence cometh my help. My help cometh from the Lord who made heaven and earth.' To drink in a mountain view helps to 'restore our soul', to use a phrase from another favourite Psalm, the twenty-third. There is, however, more behind these first two verses of Psalm 121 than is immediately apparent. They represent a development in the people of Israel's ideas about God.

As I have written elsewhere in these pages, the early Hebrews, lately escaped from their Egyptian serfdom and looking to their Promised Land, thought of their God as a local deity living up a mountain. It was up to Mount Sinai that Moses went to fetch the Ten Commandments. The gods of ancient peoples were often thought to live in high places. Mountain tops carried a deep feeling of mystery, as they still do.

In due time the people of Israel abandoned belief in a mountain God. It is as if the Psalmist is saying: 'I will lift up mine eyes to the hills. Thither was I accustomed to turn my gaze in my search for God. But does my help any longer come from the hills? No, it comes from the Lord who made heaven and earth and is not imprisoned on the top of any mountain but is near me and within me.' In these first two verses of Psalm 121 there is a hidden question. The Psalmist is saying, 'I look to the mountains.' Then he asks, 'Where will my help come from?' And then he answers the question. 'My help will come from the Lord who made heaven and earth.' Not from the mountains, he might have added.

Still, if to look to the mountains inspires thoughts of God and a sense of the spiritual, so be it.

That brave American lady, Helen Keller, mentioned in her Journal a visit she paid to the Marquis of Aberdeen during the summer before he died. They stood by his study window, and he spoke into Miss Keller's hand, as she put it. She had been blind and deaf from the age of two. 'That is Lochnagar up there,' he said, 'the mountain I look at first in the morning and last at night. Helen, Lochnagar with the golden sun on his head and the bright greenness below is like the Hills of God unto which I lift my eyes, and which I shall soon ascend.' For the Marquis, that mountain provided a focus for his prayers morning and evening. They reminded him daily of the presence of God.

Mountains and hills play a major role in the drama of our redemption. As we look up to Mount Sinai, we are reminded of God the Lawgiver and his Ten Commandments. These are the demands God imposes upon us for the right living of our days.

We look up to the mount of Transfiguration where Jesus and three of his disciples prayed, and where Peter, James and John were granted some strange psychic experience in the presence of their Master which much moved and comforted them. 'Master. how good it is that we are here,' exclaimed Peter.

And then we can look up to that green hill faraway outside the city wall where Jesus was crucified and where, by his suffering and death, in some way beyond our understanding, he built a bridge of reconciliation between God and humankind for ever.

Finally, we look up to the hill of his Ascension where he promised his followers, before he visibly departed from them, that he would be with them for ever as they went into all the world and preached the gospel.

We look to the mountains, and in a thousand ways we are reminded of God.

Mountains also stand for permanence and security. In Zimbabwe there are at least two locations known as the World's View. One is in the east in a starkly mountainous region a little reminiscent of the Scottish Highlands. From a vantage point you can view vast ranges stretching for miles. It is a majestic sight. Standing there one day, I thought of Jesus and his temptations in the wilderness. 'Then the Devil took Jesus to a very high mountain,' it says, 'and showed him all the kingdoms of this world.' Literally impossible, of course. But stand on an eminence and drink in the World's View in Zimbabwe, and you feel you're seeing all the world's kingdoms.

There's another place with the same name near Bulawayo where the grave of Cecil Rhodes may be seen. He asked to be buried there. I not only thought in those places of Jesus and his temptations. I felt the sense of sheer permanence which the mountains there seemed to represent. One felt like the author of Psalm 125 who wrote of 'The Security of God's People', the heading to the Psalm in the Good News Bible. 'As the mountains surround Jerusalem,' it says, 'so the Lord surrounds his people now and for ever.'

In this shifting and uncertain world, we need a sense of permanence and security. What strong and sure words there are in that classic hymn by the man who also gave us 'Abide with me'!

> Frail as summer's flower we flourish,
> Blows the wind and it is gone;
> But while mortals rise and perish
> God endures unchanging on.

A minister one day passed beneath the open windows of a classroom where the old-fashioned way of teaching history was in full swing. 'Tell me,' he heard the teacher say, 'tell me, what range of mountains had Napoleon to cross in order to launch his campaign in the Peninsula?' The eavesdropper couldn't catch the replies, but he did hear the teacher say with some disdain: 'Alps! The Alps, indeed! You must have Alps on the brain!' Clearly the pupil was confusing Napoleon with Hannibal. But what a phrase! Alps on the brain! We need them, if they represent ideas of permanence and security. We may see in all around us change and decay, but God abides with us, and Jesus Christ is the same yesterday, today and for ever.

Life is a climb. Spiritually, we are called to be climbers heading with sweat and toil for the heavenly heights. This, unfortunately, doesn't appeal to us. We want it easy. I do, I admit. It's been said by some wit that 'getting out of a rut is the highest mountain most of us have to climb'. Indolence and apathy are fearful enemies of human progress in every sense, and not least in spiritual growth.

The right spirit in such matters was shown by the American artist William Merritt Chase. A friend, looking at all his wonderful paintings in the studio, asked him which he considered the best. Chase walked across to a large empty canvas stretched ready in a frame and said, 'That is my best work.' Perfection in art as in life entails a climb. Anne Bronte, the youngest of the literary sisters, fed the idea into a poem.

> Believe not those who say,
>   The upward path is smooth,
> Lest thou shouldst stumble in the way
>   And faint before the truth
>
> It is the only road
>   Unto the realms of joy;
> But he who seeks that blest abode
>   Must all his powers employ

36
Round Table

The village of Dunster in Somerset sports a fine castle a millennium old. Touring it we came upon an unusual hexagonal table. Unusual not in its six-sidedness but because its top had once been the sounding-board of a pulpit in Wells Cathedral. Placed behind and above the preacher in days before microphones and public address systems were the thing, this table-top would have conserved and directed the sound of his voice to the congregation. Driving home days later, I found myself playing around with ideas arising from that sounding-board.

A round table spells *discussion*.

Maybe the fate of that sounding-board illustrates the decline in the value and quality of sermons and preaching today. The means of speaking a word from the Lord out of the Word of the Lord has been taken down and turned into a round table for discussing the faith in groups. Sermons are replaced by seminars. For a long time now, Free Church architecture has tended to push the pulpit from its central position to the side, and a table, the table of the Lord's Supper, has become the focus of the congregation's attention. A table instead of a pulpit.

Because sermons have generally become poorer in quality, and most preaching fails to compete with the high standards of professional broadcasting, the purpose of the pulpit has fallen into decline. There has also been a failure in average concentration levels. More and more people no longer believe that sermons are the thing wherein to catch consciences and save souls. When *Life* magazine devoted an entire issue to world religions including Christianity, it portrayed the typical North American Protestant minister going about his weekly duties. There he was, writing his sermon under the light of a lamp at midnight, probably on Saturday. He was depicted scrambling it together at the last moment, whereas good preaching depends on hours of preparation.

The story is told of a minister who wasn't lazy or hard-pressed but conceited. He boasted publicly that he was well able to prepare his sermon during the few minutes it took him to walk to the church from the manse nearby. In time the elders, bored by his unprepared preaching, bought him a new manse. It was five miles from the church!

People still hope for good preaching, and it can still be effective. John Perry was an Essex lad who left school in his teens and became a pop musician. He lived it up as a hell-raiser, had no time for church which bored him, and he sought fulfilment in drink, drugs and the search for 'kicks'. He was then roped in as a member of Cliff Richard's supporting group. His new job took him into many church events which he patiently and indifferently sat through, until one day he was changed. Converted, in fact.

John Perry then engaged in full-time Christian work leading the music at big evangelistic crusades. How did this change, this turnabout in direction, come about? By Sir Cliff's influence? Partly. But it was in South Africa that *he heard a sermon*. The preacher seemed, he said, to be speaking directly to if not at him. He said that it was really God speaking to him in church that day. That's what preaching is all about, and we still need awakening sermons, not their opposite.

A round table spells *equality*.

On a Friday morning in December 1984, my friend Fred Kaan settled into the 7.40 train from Coventry for the journey to Euston. On the way he jotted down the words of a hymn he was writing. We sang it at my induction five months later at Rodborough Tabernacle. Fred made the point that a round table 'has no sides or corners, no first or last, no honours ... no protocol for seating', and it's a table 'where every head is crowned'. I suspect that Fred was inspired by a poem from an anonymous source which at the time had been going the rounds among us. Its title is 'In Search of a Roundtable', and it emphasizes the essential and inevitable equality which such a structure encourages and even imposes upon us. 'It would mean no daising and throning,' wrote the unknown poet, 'for but one King is there, and He was a foot-washer, at table no less.'

The Church, infected still by the world's notions of rank and status, has its top tables for what are sometimes called its 'top brass'. The Church has been weakened by long ago inventing two classes of Christian the professional priest and the amateur lay person. In the final reckoning, we are all equal before God. Remember that story about the Duke of Wellington and the lowly estate worker who inadvertently knelt at the communion rail in the chapel right next to the Duke. Suddenly realizing his mistake, he quickly stammered his apologies and was about to withdraw when the Duke grabbed him by the arm and said: 'Stay; we are all equal here.'

The table of the Lord's Supper should really be one around which we could all literally gather, to emphasize our oneness in Christ.

In the ninth chapter of Second Samuel, there is an account of a magnanimous gesture on the part of King David. The custom of the time allowed a new king to put all of his predecessor's family to the sword. David didn't follow it. Instead, he invited Mephibosheth, the disabled son of his close friend Jonathan, to a permanent place at the royal table. 'I am no better than a dead dog, sir!' the cripple blurted out, chokingly no doubt. 'Why should you be so good to me?' David bestowed upon him an equal status with his own sons.

We too are invited to the table of the King of kings. 'You will eat and drink at my table in my Kingdom,' said Jesus to his original disciples; and there is no reason to suppose that the promise has been withdrawn. Yet even at that Last Supper, in Luke 22: 24-27. we read how they fell to arguing about status and rank. Jesus himself, head of every top table, was their Lord and Master, but also their servant. They too must exercise the authority he was giving them as servants willing to engage in lowly service, even foot-washing. So, when you and I come to the Lord's table, we come as servants of the Most High, yet paradoxically on equal terms.

Tables, round or otherwise, are *a focus for celebration*

A sweet and happy slice of musical theatre came to London some years ago from sunny Italy. Its title was *Beyond the Rainbow*, but in Italy it was *Aggiungi Un Posto A Tavola* which means 'Come join us at the table'. It was about a second Noah's Ark and was based on a novel *After Me The Deluge* by journalist David Eliades and Robert Forrest Webb, an adventure and historical novelist.

The action occurs in the fictional mountain village of San Crispino. The local priest Father Sylvestro listens incredulously as God orders him to build an ark for the saving of his community. We hear the voice of God booming and bullying from the Vaudeville theatre's 'gods'. a *deus ex electronica* supplied over the sound system. This God, who made his first man and, it was said, thereafter failed to keep a tight enough control over the production line, intends a second Deluge and another new beginning. The ark is eventually built, and in two minutes, and the rains come. So to a happy and sensational ending with the rainbow and the feast to which all are invited, with an empty chair reserved for God himself.

The closing moments of the show are its most impressive and memorable, after twenty-four scenes changed before our very eyes. They have been saved, including old Enrico, the mean atheist mayor who has all along ridiculed the priest and is almost a repetition of Guareschi's character Peppone in *The Little World of Dom Camillo*. They assemble in the village square now occupied with a long table offering enough seats for all. They sing in reprise the main musical number of the evening, 'Come join us at the table'. Entirely without the fencing with which fervent churchmen are forever wanting to surround that table, it is an invitation, without strings attached and no barriers, to sacramental fellowship. The sensation, bringing a gasp of delight from the audience, is the sudden entrance of a real live dove, immaculately circus-trained, that flies down from somewhere in the circle to perch on the back of the empty chair reserved for God at the table.

'The church is like a table, a table for a feast.' sings Fred Kaan, 'to celebrate the healing of all excluded-feeling.' The table is 'set in an open house' with 'an end to "them" and "us".'

37

Too much talk

The minister's son as a small boy was taken to a typical Protestant Reformed service conducted by his father. It was built around the sermon delivered from a large and dominant central pulpit. What did he think of it? The boy curtly replied 'Too much talk.'

We worship through words, preached, prayed, read and sung. Within the worship hour, a flood of them is poured out, mainly by the leader up front. In the beginning was the Word, and the words of the Bible enclose what we term the Word of God. The Reformers felt the need for words because Catholic worship had been submerged in mystery and even, so it seemed, in magic. Widespread ignorance had led to much superstitious dread. So, there grew up a 'lust for intelligibility', to use Bishop Hensley Henson's phrase, and there followed a torrent of words explaining things. The Protestant eagerness to convey meaning tended to obscure the essential mystery and mood in worship.

We are compelled to acknowledge that the profoundest experiences in life as well as in worship cannot be adequately conveyed in words. Aside from words though not from the Word, there are other ways of worship which are much neglected in our tradition.

For example, we may worship God through SILENCE.

An advertising executive, Godfrey Howard, told of a millionaire he knew who made his money from composing jingles for TV commercials. 'He lived in a world of tinkling pianos, tape-recorders and vocal groups,' wrote Mr Howard. 'Once when he asked me a question, there must have been a pause for all of five seconds while I thought about the answer. "What's the matter?" he demanded anxiously. "I can't stand these terrible silences!"

Maybe we feel the same way. Silence can be embarrassing. I recollect visiting several Quaker Meeting Houses during my Gloucestershire days. One evening, about seventy people from different churches sat for quite a time in silence. I didn't find it difficult. There was a calm and a serenity there which soothed us, coming as we did out of the busy, noisy clamour of Gloucester city centre. I sat there not so much absorbing the silence as waiting for someone to stand up and speak. Two or three did, eventually, and said a few words presumably as the Spirit moved them. But I, conditioned as I am against silence as an end in itself, in worship or elsewhere, found it strange. We would say, 'Jesus is Word not Silence.'

Moreover, there are times when speech may be what Dr Gordon Wakefield, a Methodist scholar, described as a 'blasphemous intrusion.' Many years ago, some friends of his lost their third and last surviving son. Letters of condolence flooded in, and their writers attempted to reconcile loss and sorrow and faith. But most help came to those shattered parents from the local vicar, who called during the summer evening before the funeral and simply stood silent at the garden gate. It was, said Dr Wakefield, a wordless act of almost total union.

A Jesuit scholar wrote: 'Our efforts to do justice to God in words are like attempts to play a Beethoven symphony on a dustbin lid.'

Perhaps we should school ourselves to include more silence in worship than we do. It says in that somewhat puzzling, sometimes weird book of Revelation that 'there was silence in heaven for about half an hour'. Couldn't we do with a regular spell like that, in the midst of bustling, frantic modern life. But half an hour's complete hear-a-pin-drop quiet in church at morning worship? Some prospect! And yet do we not need to learn how to cope with what the poet Whittier in that hymn pictured as 'the silence of eternity interpreted by love'?

We may worship God with COLOUR.

There are, did you know, instructions in the early pages of scripture about worshipping God *colourfully*. Turn up Exodus 35 and 36, and you will read what the people of Israel brought to the worship of their God in the Tent of his Presence. 'All the skilled women,' it says, 'brought fine linen thread and thread of blue, purple and red wool, which they had made.' The most skilled Israelite men, we are further told, actually made that Tent, a kind of portable church. 'They made it out of ten pieces of fine linen woven with blue, purple and red wool.' Such was the official colour combination for Israel's God.

Early in the Middle Ages, the Church produced a colour code which is still in use in the vestments worn at Mass by the priests. Altars and pulpits carry different colours for the changing seasons of the Christian year. Purple in Advent, suggesting dawn and expectation, and in Lent, another season of preparation. Green takes over for summer and autumn through those interminable Sundays after Trinity. Green spells earth, and after Easter when Christ's blood has been sown in the earth to give life to the world, green prevails. There is blue (Ash Wednesday), black (Good Friday) and white at Easter.

It's a pity that we in our churches do not change colours for these changing seasons, nor do we use them to express worship. Not that our ministers are entirely all black in their clerical attire for the sanctuary. Vestments of many colours are evident nowadays, and this is to be welcomed. One minister and his wife moved on retiring to a different locality, and one morning their local pastor called to welcome them. The husband himself was out, so it was left to the wife to meet the visitor who happened to be wearing one of his several clerical shirts. It was the bright yellow one. After he had gone, the man of the house returned, and his wife said, 'We've had a pastoral call from a canary!'

More seriously, we are called to 'worship the Lord in the beauty of holiness'. What does this mean exactly? Generally it is believed that the words refer to the sacred apparel worn by officials in the place of worship. The Good News Bible has a footnote which uses the phrase 'garments of worship'. Colour is more than hinted at, adding beauty to the worship.

In that Friends' Meeting House in Gloucester, as in other Quaker places in which I have worshipped, I haven't, I confess, cared for the building's puritan plainness and austerity. The notion, I suppose, is that there must be no distraction such as architecture and colour to divert our attention from the worship of God who is Spirit and, it is said, must be worshipped spiritually. But is colour only a distraction? Can it not be the expression of our worship of the Creator of colour?

We may worship God in MOVEMENT.

How rigid most of us are in our services. We sit in pews and stand to sing, and that's it. On the contrary, worship as depicted in Revelation is as physically active as in a gymnasium, if not exhausting. Those twenty-four elders in heaven fall down, throw their crowns down in front of the throne, throw themselves face downwards before God. All talk of people going to heaven to rest in peace may not be entirely accurate.

Imagine us, if we had no pews but an open space, doing such things on a Sunday morning. It's not our style any more than hand-clapping and the demonstrative exchange of the Peace. Colin Morris said some years ago that 'it isn't part of the life-style of the average Christian to dance down the aisle with a daffodil behind his ear'.

Fair comment. But even so, there has historically been a tradition in the Church that uses the whole body for the expression of the worship of Almighty God. The idea of a Christ as Lord of the Dance is no undesirable innovation of the 1960s. It derives from the Middle Ages, even earlier. In the fourth century when devout monks resorted to the desert to escape the vices and temptations of city life, to avoid Las Vegas as it were, they spent long hours in their little huts chanting the psalms by heart, bowing, kneeling and prostrating themselves.

In the thirteenth century, St Dominic used gestures in prayer. It was said that he made use of his body as a means of raising his soul more devoutly to the Lord above. There is a manuscript entitled St *Dominic's Nine Ways of Prayer* in which there are pictures of the saint bowing, kneeling, prostrating, genuflecting, stretching out his hands in intercession. In Seville Cathedral, the altar boys danced before the altar on Christmas Day and on other feast days. The choir boys at York did the same until the end of the sixteenth century.

Do we not need a more energetic church which in its worship delights in colour and knows how to make better use of silence?

38

Full barns in the Bible

Is material prosperity the gift from an approving God? Ask Jerry Falwell, leader of America's 'moral majority' and the evangelist who embraces the political right-wing government of George W Bush, and he will quote scripture.

The Bible lists what the Good News Bible headlines in Deuteronomy 28 as 'The Blessings of Obedience'. The writer unequivocally affirms that if the people of Israel obey the Lord their God and faithfully keep all his commands, all blessings will be theirs. Abundant crops, cattle, sheep and children will come their way.

Jerry Falwell's contention is that material wealth is, as he once said, 'God's way of blessing people who put him first'. He himself is very well off. He lives in a twelve-room Southern-style mansion with swimming pool, Bible-quoting security guards and a concrete wall eight feet high known among the wags of Lynchburg as 'the wall of Jerryco'. He receives a fat salary, free life insurance and he travels about 200,00 miles a year in a personal jet.

The writer of Proverbs paints a picture for us at Harvest Festival of full barns packed with grain, and more wine than can be stored. On the other hand, disobedience toward the Lord God, according to the Old Testament, is inevitably followed by the nemesis of crop failure and famine. The brief book of Joel, just three chapters, is about a plague of locusts that fell upon ancient Israel, followed by a terrible drought. The prophet saw the catastrophe as what lawyers technically term an 'act of God', but in this instance literally so. God was punishing his people for their sin. 'The seeds die in the dry earth,' he cried. 'There is no grain to be stored, and so the empty granaries are in ruins.'

Did the Bible writers get it right? Are full barns the certain sign of divine approval? We dare to ask these questions, and many more.

Are the poor, the hungry and those dying of malnutrition to blame for their condition?

Are all who are rich the virtuous of the world and acceptable to God, while those who are otherwise are suffering because they are disobedient to the Lord?

Questions like these must convince us that the truth is surely other than we look for it in some parts of the Old Testament. Biblical fundamentalism is both mistaken and dangerous. It leads preachers like Falwell to declare, callously and simplistically, that those on the dole in his own country, victims of the fluctuations of the economy and market forces, 'ought to be left to starve until they decide a job is a good deal'. These are his very words.

Full barns in the Bible represent *a stern warning against complacent materialism*.

Jesus manifestly did not accept the traditional view that material wealth is God's way of blessing those who put him first – whatever that means in practice. Not that he condemned earthly prosperity. He did, however, warn against it, especially in that telling tale of the rich fool. 'I will tear down my barns and build bigger ones, where I will store my corn and all my other goods,' said this man, rubbing his hands gleefully. 'Then I will say to myself, Lucky man!' But God said to him, 'You fool!' (Luke 12: 13-21)

The riches of this world are strictly temporary benefits of no value whatever in the next. Jesus wasn't against shrewd foresight and wise providence, but he didn't care much for selfish or fussy and anxious hoarding.

It has become something of a hackneyed truism, a tired cliché, to talk of the world as a global village. We are asked to imagine the world community of three billion human beings in terms of a village of a thousand. Only 164 live reasonably well, while 836 exist under varying degrees of poverty, disease, economic and political oppression, degradation and so on. 'Remember,' says someone, 'in this village of a thousand persons there is instantaneous communication. The poor are acutely aware of their plight. They have seen their neighbour's refrigerators, washers, dryers and automobiles and wonder why they are without them.' It is because of our Western overweight in the world's goodies.

The major question is whether we strive to do something about it, or remain complacently greedy, a company who are all right, Jack, full stop. Archbishop Dom Helder Camara of Brazil summed up our situation by posing two major questions. 'Which is more difficult and more exciting,' he asked: to humanize subhuman men wretched by misery, or to humanize supermen dehumanized by luxury?' To create a better world both need to be done, and urgently.

Let's consider the abundance of harvest in spiritual terms. Paul wrote of 'the harvest of the Spirit'. The hymnodist wrote of 'the harvest of beauty' for the eye to behold in nature, and of 'harvests that eye cannot see', meaning the qualities of which humankind under God is gloriously capable. But what I mean now has to do with what has been attractively described as 'the treasure of a well-stored memory'.

Benita Kyle, an expert in Christian counselling, in a talk I heard at a ministers' training conference, spoke of the value of a formal liturgy. She had attended an Anglican's girls' boarding school. Years and years later, even as her beloved husband lay dying, she drew enormous strength, she told us, from repeating to herself the Creed, the General Thanksgiving and other such pieces of the traditional liturgy she had been compelled to learn by heart in her schooldays. Those historic statements of faith and the prayers proved to be a devotional storehouse in her hour of desperate need.

Benita went on to say that if you visit The Leys School in Cambridge, a distinguished Methodist public school, they will show you John Wesley's rosary beads. A man subject to doubt and depression throughout his life despite his vibrant faith, Wesley resorted to those beads which helped him in his time of need to stay on the pathway of Christian pilgrimage.

A verse in Psalm 119 was translated by James Moffat like this: *'I store thy word within my heart.'* We need that treasure of a well-stored memory for the dark days. The trouble is that learning things by rote, except for actors, is out of fashion. The only things we remember now are catchphrases in TV shows and advertising slogans. Even the 23rd Psalm and the Lord's Prayer are fading from memory. And despite the fair spate of hymn-singing on TV and radio, most young brides and bridegrooms haven't a clue about hymns. How will they fare in time of crisis and need, their mental barns empty or containing only tat?

Full barns in the Bible underline the *obligation to share God's bounty.*

The noteworthy thing about Joseph in the Old Testament isn't his Amazing Technicolor Dreamcoat, but his compassion and generosity. He is rescued from a well and ends up as top man in Egypt. He foresees the seven years of famine, and he makes arrangements for the stockpiling of food throughout the land during the previous seven years of plenty.

The hungry people of adjoining lands come to him to bale them out by doling out supplies to them. Joseph's brothers come begging. They had treated him badly, but he didn't refuse them. He gave orders that their packs were to be filled with corn, that they were to be given their money back and food for the return journey. He had full barns but also a rich supply of compassion and generosity. He accepted without question the obligation to share God's bounty.

'Whoever has food must share it,' said John the Baptist centuries later. To share is the demand that Jesus Christ lays upon us. This is the final message of the Bible's full barns.

Here are words by Fred Kaan in a hymn for harvest translated from the German of Dieter Trautwein.

> *Blessing shrivels up when your children hoard it;*
> *Help us, Lord, to share, for we can afford it;*
> *blessing only grows in the act of sharing….*

39

The flags on the fort

I met a man on the Common walking his dog. He poked his walking stick in the direction of the Fort and expressed a red-faced angry disapproval. 'You mean, the Japanese flag?' I asked him. 'Well, we fought the French once,' I added. 'We're still fighting them,' he snorted. The Japanese flag was flapping gently in the south-west breeze on the Fort tower. Some of his friends, he explained, had suffered horribly at the hands of the Japs during the war. 'Anyway,' he went on, 'we don't want people like that living round here.'

He was referring to the somewhat eccentric owner of Rodborough Fort, which stood on the edge of the Common and was part of my pastoral catchment area just above Stroud in 1988. Jo had proved something of an irritant to the local community since moving in among us early in the previous year. The dog-walking gentleman with the florid complexion obviously didn't know that she had spent £3000 on refurbishing the chapel in the Fort; and she was encouraging its use for worship, although her bank manager preferred the idea of converting it into a bar. He warned her that his bank wouldn't at any price help to finance a chapel.

More in sorrow than in anger, I walked away, trailing our own two Tibetan dogs. I thought ahead to One World Week in October, for this was early August. I had, I suspected, been speaking to a typical Englishman of Gilbertian comic opera whose home was his castle. Let the drawbridge be pulled up, for all outside must be enemies. To him, only the Union Jack should be flown above any fort in England's green and pleasant land. Most other flags were almost certainly unacceptable, and many were anathema.

The owner of Rodborough Fort had acquired over thirty national flags, and she believed that she should exhibit them in turn to demonstrate her own 'one world' beliefs. What if you or I were in her place? Would we fly the Japanese flag? I've had friends in former congregations who had suffered under Japanese cruelty in the wartime camps. Today I am indebted to Japan for much of my excellent electronic machinery. Would you put the Irish republican flag on your tower. One could name other flags of other nations who seem inimical to us. The Fort's owner admitted that she might be wiser to place the UN flag over her Fort. Or, if you like, an array of several national flags together. Better than any one on its own, sticking out like the proverbial sore thumb, and inviting adverse comment from dog-walkers on the Common, or over the phone from local residents much offended; or even, as it turned out, in the national press.

Those who hold the view that many of the world's problems arise from religious convictions are, sad to say, right. Can we, should we, say to anyone, 'You're not one of us'? Are there, ought there to be, lines drawn separating us all into 'them and us' groups?

The first disciples of Jesus were inclined to be exclusive brethren. One of them, John, consulted him about a man they'd seen casting out demons. 'We told him to stop,' John said, 'because he doesn't belong to our group.' So, what does Jesus say? He says: 'Do not try to stop him ... For whoever is not against us is for us.'(Mark 9: 38-40)

Writing to his fellow-Christians in Galatia, Paul laid it down without compromise. He said: 'There is no difference between Jews and Gentiles, between slaves and free men, between men and women; you are all one in union with Christ Jesus.' (Galatians 3: 38) A revolutionary axiom, this, and one into which the human race has yet to enter fully, and which hasn't been taken up even within the Christian fold.

We Christians still draw lines of mutual hatred *denominationally*.

In Limavady, County Londonderry, on Christmas Day 1983, the Revd David Armstrong wished his fellow-clergyman Father Kevin Mullan a happy Christmas. For making that generous gesture of friendship between fellow-Christians, David was branded a traitor by his own congregation. He received threatening phone calls and letters. It was only because David was a Protestant and Kevin a Catholic (I refuse to insist that he should be described as a *Roman* Catholic, true though it is, but it sounds so bigoted).

Two years earlier, a bomb had blown up the Catholic church opposite David's Presbyterian building. At once he condemned those responsible. Within hours he was getting phone calls from Protestant extremists openly declaring that they were only too sorry there hadn't been Catholics inside so that the roof would have fallen in on them.

It should be said that there were many parishioners in both churches who welcomed David Armstrong's compassionate and reconciling attitude, but most of them were too scared to say so openly. The threats grew louder and more bloodthirsty. More phone calls came saying that they would throw the Armstrong children on the orange fire. For offering the hand of Christmas friendship and greeting across the road, David was censured by his elders who demanded his resignation. In the end he and his family had to flee not only from his church but from Northern Ireland. He sought refuge with the Church of England in Oxford where he was offered a post and the family provided with accommodation at a secret address.

I cannot claim that such a case is typical. We only hear the extreme 'man-bites-dog' stories about the activities of fanatics and extremists. But it shows how far we have yet to go to get away from the hate that still exists among us Christians.

We Christians still draw lines of exclusion *theologically*.

When Billy Graham arrived in this country to conduct *Mission England*, he received a letter from Pastor Jack Glass and his followers in Glasgow. You may be excused for thinking that Graham and Glass belong roughly to the same school of thought, both being fundamentalist evangelical Protestants. Glass wrote: 'I feel it is my duty as a minister of the gospel to accuse you of being the biggest traitor to Christ since Judas Iscariot. By your pro-Rome ecumenical evangelism you demolished the wall of separation from apostasy built at the Protestant

Reformation.' He went on to accuse Billy Graham of being 'the Pope's puppet and the "evangelical" monkey of the ecumenical organ-grinders'. It is hard to suppress laughter at this.

Among extremist Protestants. 'ecumenical' is a dirty word. I apologise for sharing these sorry cases of hate and hostility with you. Perhaps I am wrong to do so, but how far off we are from the teaching of Jesus and Paul's conviction that we are all one in union with Christ Jesus.

On the day after my encounter with that man and his dog on Rodborough Common, a Swiss flag was flying on the Fort. Who could possibly object to that? Switzerland has kept out of the wars, although it is a country well prepared to cope with the attack of an enemy. Every Swiss male remains a soldier for thirty years, on call at any time and required to do up to two months of military training every year. He keeps his rifle at home together with ammunition and his uniform. Every new building put up must have an air-raid shelter beneath it. The Swiss are realistic people who know that they live in a dangerous world where they, as all of us, are bound to have enemies.

Jesus himself acknowledged the presence of enemies, for he commanded us to love them. He gave himself on the cross to demonstrate the illimitable power and utter comprehensiveness of that love. The cross is the symbol of blood-red sacrifice for the reconciliation of the world to God, and of man to man. The Swiss flag presents us, as it flies above the Fort, with a white cross on a red background. This could well be the flag of a united humanity.

40

The monk in the chapel

Let me tell you about the monk in the chapel. They noticed that he spent long hours there, alone as well as with the others. He would be there, kneeling before the crucifix, gazing up at the face of his Saviour. They asked him about his seemingly excessive devotions. 'Well, it's like this,' he replied. 'When I go into the chapel, at first there's just *Me*. Then, after a while, there's *Me* and *Him*. But then, there's *Him* and *Me*. In the end, there's just *Him*.'

'While I was with you,' Paul said to his Corinthian friends, 'I made up my mind to forget everything except Jesus Christ and especially his death on the cross.' (I Corinthians 2: 2) That's a tall order, if it's meant literally. We've a ladder of devotion to climb before we reach anywhere near such dizzy heights. Let's company with the monk in the chapel.

'At first, there's just *Me*.'

'You have an ego – a consciousness of being an individual,' declared Billy Graham. 'But that doesn't mean that you are to worship yourself, to think constantly of yourself, and to live entirely for self.' Yet that's how some of us live all the while. Not that it's easy to live otherwise. Daily life is a constant struggle against the incessant demands of an insatiable ego; which is why we need to spend some time each day in our chapel, whatever form that chapel takes.

There is nothing worse for us human beings nor more destructive than to live entirely for self. Sir Walter Scott expressed it eloquently and devastatingly in *The Lay of the Last Minstrel* when he wrote about patriotism.

The wretch, concentred all in self
Living, shall forfeit fair renown,
And, doubly dying, shall go down,
To the vile dust, from whence he sprung
Unwept, unhonoured, and unsung

Or, for a contemporary comment, let's turn to Sam King, a post-war immigrant from the West Indies who became Mayor of Southwark. He summed up our country in a sentence. He told a Fleet Street reporter, 'A third of the British people are still neo-Fascists, a third are really responsible, nice people, and a third don't care about anything so long as there is beer in the pubs.' Not a precise sociological analysis of our population, but it will do for now.

Possibly the worst form of self-centredness is self-pity. Some poor folk are grumblers from start to finish, moaners from cradle to grave. Even beyond, according to one joker of a minister long since departed this scene. Ernest Gould of Chelmsford was a cracker for wit and jokes. He used to say to a small congregation in a large building with rows of empty pews that the main family present was the wood family. We're discussing perennial complainers, which reminded me of Ernest and the many broadcast talks he gave on 'Lift Up Your Hearts', an early predecessor of today's 'Thought for the Day' on BBC Radio 4. In one of them he imagined one perennial moaner wailing even in heaven: 'Me halo's too tight, me harp's out of tune, and the cloud I'm sitting on is damp.'

'After a while, there's *Me* and *Him*.'

Self interest may continue to prevail even in the presence of the crucified and risen Lord. Sensitive Christians of bygone times were wont to ask the question put by a trembling jailer to the two missionaries, Paul and Silas: 'Sirs, what must I do to be saved?' Earth tremors had dislodged the prison doors and unshackled the prisoners in custody at Philippi. The jailer, seeing the doors busted open, assumed that his inmates were out and free; and this meant only one thing, namely that he would be held responsible and executed. He had his sword out and was about to commit suicide when Paul shouted: 'Don't harm yourself! We are all here.' The poor man nonetheless felt that he was still in

---

trouble. When he asked what he should do to be saved, he didn't mean from the fires of hell but from harsh Roman justice. Paul, quick as lightning, turned his question to a profounder use. And that's how we interpret the question now (Acts 16).

Congregations today, at least in our tradition, are probably more conscious of doubt than of guilt. If we feel guilty, it is likely to be about what we eat and drink to make us overweight rather than about the sins we commit to bring the wrath of God down upon our heads. Doctors more than priests create to-day's guilt-edged society. Past generations, however, were sometimes eaten up with fear and foreboding about their eternal fate. I have ministered to old men dying scared of what awaited them beyond their last breath. They were exclusively preoccupied with concern for their personal salvation. The big question asked by Christian in *The Pilgrim's Progress* is what he must do to be saved. That, in those days, was the question to haunt a man as he read his Bible. Moreover, we note that Christian was prepared to walk out on his own wife and family to gain his own salvation.

Church historian Geoffrey Nuttall observed that the age in which Bunyan lived saw the birth of self-consciousness on a grand scale. It was the age of Rembrandt who painted self-portraits, of Descartes whose philosophy was summed up in the historic phrase *cogito ergo sum*, 'I think, therefore I exist'; and people kept diaries and wrote autobiographies. They were all too liable to be over-concerned with their own souls. Today, we are not urgently asking what we must do to be saved. We want to know how to achieve self-fulfillment. In another form, the self prevails.

I wonder how many of us come to church for a spiritual 'fix', for personal consolation rather than salvation, for comfort more than challenge, to be ministered to rather than to minister, and to receive help for themselves rather than to learn how to share in mission and evangelism, is it a case of Me and *Him*, but still mainly *Me?*

But then, there's *Him and Me.'*

Here is a tremendous step forward; or should I say, upward on the ladder of devotion. Look at John the Baptist. He affirmed that he himself must grow smaller while the Christ grew greater; he must become less and less while the Christ must become more and more (John 3: 30). This is what Dr James S Stewart, the renowned Scottish preacher, described as 'The heroism of self-effacement', the title of one of his sermons. He added that if John the Baptist had never spoken another word in Scripture but this, it would have marked him down as a saint.

Max is one of our grandsons, a teenager in Cheshire. His mother Liz is an Anglo-Polish Catholic, and she and her husband Richard, our own youngest, agreed that their first-born son should be named Maximilian. It was in honour of Father Maximilian Kolbe, a modern-day Saint. He was imprisoned in a Nazi concentration camp, and there came a day when he showed compassion and courage on a grand scale.

A prisoner had escaped, and the camp commandant ordered as a warning to all inmates that ten men would be starved to death. One of them was a young man with wife and children. Father Kolbe stepped out of the line and volunteered to take his place. During the ensuing weeks, Kolbe the priest prepared others for death. He himself was the last to die. In his cell there was a picture of Jesus that he had scratched on the wall with his nails. Jesus must have been his inspiration. Jesus and Maximilian Kolbe, but Jesus first.

Now, back we go for a final word from our monk in the chapel.

'In the end, there's just Him.'